The Three Rs of Investing

Return, Risk and Relativity

$

The Three Rs of Investing
Return, Risk and Relativity

Austin S. Donnelly

DOW JONES-IRWIN
Homewood, Illinois 60430

This publication is designed to provide accurate and
authoritative information in regard to the subject matter
covered. It is sold with the understanding that the
publisher is not engaged in rendering legal, accounting, or
other professional service. If legal advice or other expert
assistance is required, the services of a competent
professional person should be sought.

*From a Declaration of Principles jointly adopted by a Committee
of the American Bar Association and a Committee of Publishers.*

ISBN 0-87094-557-2

Library of Congress Catalog Card No. 84-72830

Printed in the United States of America

2 3 4 5 6 7 8 9 0 K 2 1 0 9 8 7 6 5

To **Stuart H. Struck**

In appreciation of good advice,
helpful guidance, and firm friendship

Preface

The keen observer of the investment scene today can see some signs of the same type of problem that is facing educators: the need to get back to the three Rs. In the investment field, the three Rs are return, risk, and relativity—basically simple concepts that have tended to become obscured as analysts, investment advisers, and institutions have become more and more involved in sophisticated techniques that fail to give adequate attention to the basics.

For example, in the euphoria on Wall Street in the spring of 1983, when the Dow Jones Industrial Index rose above 1200, there seemed to be tacit agreement that the law of gravity had been repealed, and that the golden age of an ever-rising stock market had arrived. Yet, a study of the relative cost of equities at that time (the cost of equities compared with fixed interest investments) showed clearly that the prospects of a better economy and improved corporate earnings had probably been overanticipated by the market. Research showed that on the basis of past experience there was only about 1 chance in 16 of the market providing enough capital gain in the next five years to enable an equity investor to break even with a bond investor (after allowing for income and capital gain tax).

The realism gap has widened considerably in recent years. That is the gap between the prices at which common stock and other equities have been selling and the lower price which would be justified on the more realistic assessment of cost of money and returns available elsewhere.

This book attempts to bring the study of investment back to fundamentals through a study of return, risk, and relativity that shows many widely accepted concepts to be invalid. It also includes the results of many years of research into the record of the stock market in achieving various levels of capital gain—and the impact of relative cost at time of investment on medium-term results.

As 29 years of varied investment experience have convinced me that no single approach provides a magic recipe for instant riches, the material in this text is not put forward as some form of modern-day financial alchemy. But the approach is a big improvement on much of the conventional investment wisdom. It includes the application to investment decisions of the opportunity cost concept, which has been widely used in business management.

I would like to acknowledge valuable assistance from a number of people—Mr. Stuart H. Struck (to whom the book is dedicated); Dr. Peter Struck; Merrill Lynch, Pierce, Fenner & Smith; Citi Investments; Bateman Eichler Hill Richards; and my son Dr. P. J. Donnelly. In expressing my sincere thanks to them for their assistance in various ways, including the provision of information and comments, I would point out that the views expressed in the text are my own.

Austin S. Donnelly

Contents

concept. Effect of currency changes on foreign investments. Some nonfinancial factors. A summary of Part 2.

PART 3—The Second R—Risk in Investing 59

PART 5—Practical Aspects of Day-by-Day Investment Decisions   129

sector of the economy. Market-oriented factors. Factors affecting particular stocks. Indicators favorable to the stock market. Indicators unfavorable to the stock market. The problem of mixed indicators. Short-term trading. Preferred stock. Convertible notes.

part 1

Introduction

1

Introduction

A steward on a ship who had been given a bottle of liquor by a passenger was asked by his friend what it was like. He replied that it was "just right"—explaining that if it had been any better it would have not have been given to him, and if it had been any worse it would not have been drinkable.

One of the biggest reasons for investment losses o. disappointing results is assuming that a market (stock market, real estate market, or commodity market) is just right at a particular time. For example, in the stock market rise of 1982–83, claims were made that the market must continue to go up because interest rates were declining and the U.S. economy was recovering, or about to recover.

The serious weakness in these arguments was that they assumed that the market was just right when those comments were made. In fact, the cost of stocks at that time, relative to other investments, was considerably higher than it had been for most of the previous three decades. Hence, the benefits of falling interest rates and an improving economy were fully anticipated, and probably overanticipated, in the market price (one reason being that in the previous two years, prices had not moved downward to the extent that would be necessary to reflect the lower prices then needed to provide a higher income yield in line with the increases in interest rates at that time).

Departure from the Three Rs

In the spring of 1983, there was a lot of discussion in the United States of the findings of the commission on the educational system. The findings showed that despite a very large increase in the money spent on education, the system was producing students who were less literate and less numerate than in earlier years. Many people saw this as being the result of the education system drifting too far away from the three Rs ("reading, 'riting, and 'rithmetic"). They saw this as being at least partly due to inadequate attention to the fundamentals.

In stock markets and, indeed, in most other investment markets there has also been a tendency to depart from fundamentals. There has been the paradox of ever more sophisticated means of making a wide variety of investments and of obtaining information about investments accompanied by far less realism in markets than 30 years ago.

Thirty years ago, when investment markets were a good deal less sophisticated, the average dividend yield on common stocks was 5.9 percent (1953). That was well above the Moody's Aaa bond yield of 3.2 percent. In those days, the more practical, commonsense view tended to prevail. Because of the greater risk involved in common stocks (especially due to market fluctuation), the income return would need to be higher than that available from lower investments. In 1983, the average dividend yield of a little over 4 percent was significantly less than half the bond rate figure of 11 to 11.5 percent. As the figures later in this text clearly demonstrate, except for those wise enough or fortunate enough to take advantage of the sharp upward swings in the market, capital gain produced in the medium term—for example, a five-year period—in the stock market in the previous 10 years had been disappointing. So rational prospects of capital gain were certainly not the answer for the vast difference in those figures.

What Are the Three Rs of Investing?

The drift from reality in investing is really a drift from recognition and assessment of the following items:

1. Return—the overall return comprising income plus capital gain or minus capital loss.
2. Risk—assessment of the risk of investments, including volatile market fluctuations which can mean that "good investments," including so-called blue chips, are exposed to high risk.
3. Relativity—assessing the prices and prospects of investments relative to other available investments in deciding whether a particular investment is attractively priced or not under current conditions.

In some ways, the problem is that when attention is given to the above matters, it is often given in a superficial manner. For example, much of the literature about the stock market concentrates a great deal of attention on the return from the investment, in terms of the earnings of the company. But the investor has to realize that the undistributed portion of company earnings (the portion not distributed as dividends but retained by the company) is not automatically received by a purchaser of stock. Whether, and to what extent, a purchaser derives any benefits from retained earnings depends on a whole host of factors including changes in market cycles, changes in interest rates or the attractions of other investments, inflow or outflow of speculative funds, and changes in investment fashions, as well as the future earnings trend of the company.

Similarly, in relation to risk, the conventional wisdom does pay some attention to this question—for example, by suggesting a spread of investment to reduce the overall risk in the portfolio. This approach is certainly desirable but is not all that has to be done. If you have a well-spread portfolio invested in common stock, you are still exposed to considerable risk, mainly the risk that the whole market could fall and cause capital loss (or rise at a rate which is insufficient to give you the capital gain needed to justify that investment).

Outline of This Book

An outline of the book at this stage may be helpful. It is comprised of six parts. The introduction covers financial fables and folklore and a program for successful investing. Part 2 deals with the first of the three Rs, return, covering matters such as basic but not well understood facts about return, the time value of money and compounding, fixed and variable income, the possible sources of capital gain (which is the second element in return), and the impact of taxation on investment return.

The second of the three Rs, risk, is discussed in Part 3, which covers more obvious and less obvious sources of risk; the paradox of high risk in "good" investments, different risk categories for various investors and types of investment; the impact of borrowing on investment risk, and means of controlling, reviewing, and reducing risk. As for the third R, relativity in investing, Part 4 commences with the need to relate all investments to some standard, the principle of relativity, and the opportunity cost concept. It proceeds to consider how relative costs of common stocks have varied over the years and the impact of relative cost on investment results. It concludes with chapters on calculation of capital gain targets, the record of the market in achieving various levels, and the need to see relativity and relative cost figures in correct perspective.

Having covered the three Rs, the text proceeds, in Part 5, to practical aspects of day-by-day investment decisions. The first two chapters in this part cover basic principles including the need for investment policy and strategy, market cycles, market fashions, and the timing of investments. This is followed by a chapter on investing in bonds and lower risk investments, two chapters on the stock market, two on real estate investments, and a chapter on gold, silver, futures trading, and other investments. There are also chapters on the use of specialist managers, mutual funds, and investment aspects of buying a home. Part 6 deals with personal money management, including the wise use of credit and borrowed funds, providing for retirement, and the merits of paying off long-term debts early. In the last chapter, there is a brief summary of the book and a list of investment terms (some of them in a lighter vein, which may be worth remembering).

2

Financial Fables, Fallacies, and Folklore

In his famous book *The General Theory of Employment*, the late Lord Keynes (who was a very successful investor as well as a noted economist) included a chapter on investment and capital markets. The chapter contained this very significant statement:

Speculators may do no harm as bubbles on a steady stream of enterprise. But the position is serious when enterprise becomes the bubbles on a whirlpool of speculation. When the capital development of a country becomes the by-product of the activities of a casino, the job is likely to be ill-done.

Recently, experienced finance executives in various countries have referred to corporations being taken over in a casino-like atmosphere of the stock exchange. The increase of over 50 percent in stock prices in the United States between August 1982 and May 1983 also illustrates the way in which speculation can distort normal market movements. By no stretch of the imagination could predictions of the improvement in the U.S. economy and the decline in interest rates justify such a large rise—especially, as pointed out earlier, when the market was at a high figure relative to other investments prior to that rise.

How Fallacies Tend to Be Regarded as Facts

If a statement which is untrue or inaccurate is repeated often enough over a long enough period by enough people, it tends to be regarded as accurate. Some fallacious statements about investments have been repeated for so long that there is almost a tendency for them to be regarded as self-evident truths.

The first step for any serious investor is to realize that many of the statements which are confidently made by people in the investment world may be inaccurate, untrue, or seriously misleading. Indeed, a cynic would say that there is an inverse relationship between the confidence with which a statement is made and the reliability of that statement. It is certainly true that experienced professional investment advisers, fully aware of uncertainties in investments, normally refrain from making the exuberant, overenthusiastic claims of many newcomers to the industry— or those who are mainly concerned with making a quick dollar.

The Hedge against Inflation Fallacy

Probably the most widespread fallacy in the investment world is that there are certain investments which are a hedge against inflation, and that those investments will provide enough capital gain to offset the effects of inflation. The fact of the matter is that there is no such thing as an inflation hedge in that sense. To be an inflation hedge (remembering that the word *hedge* implies some certainty), an investment would need to provide assured gain. Some investors who bought investments at the right time and sold at the right time may have achieved more than sufficient capital gain to offset the effects of inflation. But there is no investment that can be bought at any time and any price which will always provide enough sustained gain to offset the effects of inflation. This is not possible primarily because of the words of wisdom attributed to a person not normally quoted in investment discussions, Abraham Lincoln, who said that you cannot fool all of the people all of the time.

Bigger Fool Theory

Talking of fools, it is often said that when a boom is "on the boil" in stocks or real estate, gold, or any other market, it can be a wise move to buy at a foolish price. You could make a profit by buying at a foolish price, because before too long an even bigger fool will come along and offer you an even more foolish price. I have been pointing out for some time that the one big flaw in this theory is that we live in a finite world, and the supply of fools is not limitless. So the smart thing is to ensure that you are *no later than the next-to-last fool when the crunch comes and the market goes into a serious slump.*

Thy Myth about the Magic of Gold

When gold was selling at $850 an ounce, lots of investment people who should have known better were saying that in times of high inflation it was necessary to put your funds into "hard currency" such as gold. As prices are now about 50 percent below that level over three years later, the only thing hard about that particular currency was the hard luck suffered by those who bought at that time.

Gold was described as the ultimate store of value. But how can any commodity be regarded as a store of value, let alone the ultimate store of value, if it has become the plaything of speculators and has the unstable, volatile price movements of the gold market? Remember the statements that so long as "governments are printing money," then inflation will continue, and the price of gold must rise. Those statements suggested that there was an automatic link between rates of inflation and the price of gold. In fact, in the last three years inflation has probably totaled 15 percent or more in most major countries, yet gold has declined by over 50 percent.

Myths and Fallacies in the Stock Market

As the stock markets are widely publicized and more widely studied than many other markets, it is not surprising that this is an area where myths and fallacies abound. One is the claim that you can't go wrong in buying sound stocks.

Another of the most serious and widely publicized fallacies is that of the so-called blue chip stocks. That term implies to the average investor that they are some sort of a safe haven for funds. Yet, examination shows that volatile market movements have made these stocks high risk investments. It may be true to describe certain companies as blue chip companies because of their size, financial strength, earning trends, and other desirable features. But there is no such thing as a *blue chip stock* in the commonly accepted sense of that term.

Yet another fallacy is that of the growth stock. There is no such thing as a growth stock in the commonly accepted sense of that term—a stock which is sure to produce good results in the medium and long term regardless of when, and at what price, it was bought. The facts are that even in those few cases where earnings continue to grow indefinitely, stock prices are almost sure to decline at some stage, probably in reaction to previous sharp rises.

For years many people were persuaded to invest in the stock market because stock brokers, investment advisers, finance writers, and others stated that inflation must be good for stock prices. This argument stated that as inflation pushed up the value of assets of a company and the earnings in money terms, that should be reflected in stock prices. In 1983, with inflation in the United States down to very low levels, those same people are now putting forward the argument that low inflation is good for the stock market. They support their argument by pointing out that at times in the past when inflation was low, the stock market performed very well.

One interesting point is the ability of so many of these people to turn 180° in their arguments, suddenly changing from a statement that high inflation is good for the stock market to one where low inflation or no inflation is beneficial. The other interesting point is that the earlier claim about inflation being good for the market is incorrect. If all other things had been equal, there might have been some truth in it. But other things were not equal. Earlier excessive enthusiasm for stock prices had pushed them up to higher levels, from which reaction was almost inevitable. The result was that there have been periods of high inflation accompanied by falling rather than rising stock prices. Another point is that if there is high inflation, there is a tendency for interest rates to rise. To the extent that stock prices may at least partly reflect the higher returns available elsewhere, this could also mean downward pressure on prices.

As for the claim that low inflation or no inflation is good for stock prices, that statement is also subject to some doubt. The circumstances which have produced low inflation in the United States include unemployment (and hence reduced spending power by the community), unused capacity (with only about 70 percent of capacity being used in the spring of 1983), and reduced activity in business expansion. None of those factors of themselves are good for the stock market. They could offset benefits that come from lower inflation, including lower interest rates and a reduced burden in carrying inventories, compared to the days of rapidly increasing prices.

Fallacies in Real Estate

In real estate perhaps the greatest fallacy is that real estate values never go down. In some countries real estate people say that if they stop rising they simply stabilize. If you are preparing a glossary of real estate terms, you could include in it an entry to the effect that, in the jargon of those people, stabilization means that the bottom has dropped out of the market.

Another fallacy in relation to property investment is that location is all-important—the old saying that there are three rules of which the first is location, the second is location, and the third is location. Certainly location is important, but so too is timing. Many millions have been lost through investment in *well-located investments at the wrong time*—at inflated prices just before a slump.

Another fallacy which has probably led to many unsuccessful decisions to venture into the property market is the statement that so long as inflation continues, rising replacement costs will mean an increase in value of property. That statement, which appears attractive at first sight, is invalid. Property values are not set in some cost plus formula in relation to replacement costs, but as the result of supply and demand. Oversupply and/or reduced demand in a period following a boom can often result in a substantial decline in property values at a time when replacement costs are increasing.

The Greatest Fallacy of All—the Efficient Markets Fallacy

The attitude that "my mind is made up—don't try to confuse me with the facts" is relevant in relation to capital markets, especially stock markets. Despite all the evidence of distortion in capital markets, some investment people still seriously believe in the efficient markets theory. A generation of security analysts in some business schools have been trained in this serious fallacy.

The Essence of the Fallacy and Its Errors

Oversimplifying a little, the efficient market theory says that as information about markets, especially stock markets and listed stocks, is readily available and widely publicized, information is quickly absorbed in prices. Hence, so the theory goes, nothing is to be gained by security analysis as to the stocks which may perform better. The theory would also suggest that attempts to time moves into and out of the market are not worthwhile.

The theory sounds attractive at first sight. Indeed, I once referred to the arguments supporting it as being *mathematically elegant, logically consistent, formally attractive, right answers to the wrong questions.*

If all investment decisions were based on the objective assessment envisaged by the theory, then it may be somewhere close to the mark. But a lot of investment decisions are made because of the great enthusiasm or rank despair of the moment, or because investors are persuaded by well-presented recommendations of a stock by brokers or investment advisers, or by staff submissions to management of institutions. Some examples of the difference between the realities of the marketplace and the claims of the efficient market fallacy are set out below:

1.   The figures in Chapters 19 to 21 show that over many five-year periods, common stocks, instead of earning a higher return than bonds that an efficient market would be expected to provide to compensate for the higher risk, in fact earned smaller amounts, including many periods of significant capital loss (primarily due to reaction to unrealistically high prices at time of purchase in speculative booms).

2.   The rise of over 100 percent in high technology stocks followed by a decline of about 50 percent in the 1982 to 1984 period, and the overall rise of about 50 percent in the share market between August 1982 and April 1983, when new economic information was becoming available during that period, would not have justified anything like that amount of movement.

3.   Despite the fact that for much of 1983 and the early months of 1984 the stock market was at very high levels relative to other investments, and at these levels stocks were highly unlikely (on the basis of past experience) to perform as well as bonds, nearly all investment advice (and hence most investment decisions) assumed that the market was reasonably priced.

4.   The volatility of stock prices, including rises or falls of as much as 5 to 10 percent within a matter of a few week (or days), is inconsistent with an efficient market in which such extreme movements would be unlikely.

5.   Claims by efficient market theory supporters that common stocks always do better than bonds in the long term are invalid for these reasons:

   a.   The careful selection of periods to support the argument—for example, one publication using efficient market theory to promote the sale of common stocks showed results for 57 years, 5 years, and 3 years (an odd combination), which ignored results for many other periods such as 8, 10, or 15 years, which would have given markedly different results.

   b.   Instead of comparing stock market results with earnings of low risk medium-term bonds (the effect of interest rate changes on capital value is minimized in bonds with no more than five years to maturity), the comparison is made with long-term bonds which a low risk investor seeking an alternative from the stock market would avoid like the plague, because the susceptibility of longer term bonds to serious loss of capital value arising from interest rate changes makes them a medium risk investment.

6.   By concentrating most of their comments on the stock market and considering the risk of individual stocks against the market, the efficient market supporters tend to overlook the fact that the stock market is a medium to high risk area because of volatile market movements.

7. The pronounced cyclical pattern of the stock market (see comments in Chapter 24) is inconsistent with the claims of an efficient market. If stock markets were even moderately efficient, there would be reduced buying and some selling as prices moved significantly above realistic levels (and the reverse when they moved well below those levels), which would result in far less step rises and falls than in fact occur.

Further Reading on the Efficient Market Theory

For those who are interested in further study of this subject, the following references may be helpful:

1. Vickers, Douglas. *Financial Markets in the Capitalist Process.* Philadelphia: University of Pennsylvania Press, 1978.
2. Wood. J. Stuart. "Heterogeneous Expectations and Security Price Distributions: Random Movements, Fat Tails, and Unstable Beta's." In *Proceedings of the Fourteenth Annual Meeting,* Bruce D. Fielitz, ed., pp. 144–45. Presented at the Eastern Finance Association Annual Meeting, Atlanta, Georgia, April 21, 1978.

3

A Program for Successful Investing Today

"Ours is a nonprofit organization," said a business executive. He then added ruefully: "We didn't plan it that way, that's just how it worked out." Some investment portfolios are poorly balanced with inappropriate investments, but not because people set out to build up that type of portfolio. Rather, they end up that way simply because there is no definite plan and the portfolio "just happened that way." Portfolios develop along certain lines because certain types of investments were strongly recommended at the time when funds were available.

Key Elements in an Investment Program

The key elements in an investment program today are:

A definite plan—all decisions to be made within the framework of the overall plan.

Rational approach—based on analysis of the pros and cons of various investments and facts rather than the fallacies discussed in the previous chapter.

The three Rs—proper attention to:
   a. return on investment.
   b. risk of investment.
   c. relativity of various investments.

A sound policy—investing in terms of a policy suitable to each individual investor.

Strategy—an appropriate strategy for putting policy into effect in the face of current investment market realities.

Management—organizing selection, review, and control of investments.

The portfolio effect—remember that it is the effect of an investment decision on the overall portfolio that really counts.

Money management—coordinating one's investment plan with overall money management plans.

Those are by no means the only questions which investors need to consider. But they are key elements in any program for sound investing, especially under current conditions.

The Need for a Sound Program

Some people who are in their 60s or 70s initially would be inclined to disagree with the need for a program emphasizing the elements outlined above. They may have done very well over the years, especially if they had funds to invest 20 or 30 years ago. *Conditions today and probably in the foreseeable future are not likely to be as favorable for investors as they were 20 or 30 years ago.* In those days the investment tide in popular investments, such as common stocks and real estate, was so favorable that it was possible to do well without much attention to any of the key elements now needed for successful investment.

The need for a sound program under today's conditions can be seen by looking at the stock market. In May 1983, even after the rise of over 50 percent in the previous nine months, the Dow Jones Industrial Index was only 38 percent higher than in December 1969. That means a compound growth of only 2.3 percent per annum. That figure is well below the capital gain needed to keep pace with inflation or to provide a higher return, which is needed to compensate for the extra risk (especially of market fluctuation) in common stock investments. (Nine months later stock prices had recorded a net decline of 9 percent.) By contrast, in the previous 14 years the Dow Jones Index had increased by about 258 percent, a compound rate of growth of about 9.5 percent per annum.

Certainly, those who were wise enough or lucky enough to move into the market at the low point just before the 1982 rise and who sold before the subsequent decline would have done very well. So too would investors who may have taken advantage of other sharp upswings in the market in recent years. But the point is that a large number of investors do not have the funds, skills, experience, and temperament to become successful stock traders. For the vast majority of investors, in the less favorable investment conditions of recent years it is very important that they work along sound lines in making their investment decisions.

Later chapters in the text specifically deal with many of the points outlined above, especially Parts 2, 3, and 4 dealing with return, risk, and relativity. Brief introductory comments on some of the other matters are set out below.

Investment Policy

The first important step for each investor is to consider such things as age group, income situation, cash needs, and attitude toward risk taking. The investor who is retired or close to the end of his or her working life generally has to be more conservative, less venturesome in his or her policy than would have been appropriate in earlier years. In earlier years, there would have been a chance to rebuild capital after any serious investment reversal out of savings of subsequent years.

An investor with a large amount of capital can be more venturesome with at least part of that capital than a person with limited funds to invest. The loss of some capital that could be extremely serious for the small investor may be little more than a trifling disappointment for an investor with a large amount of capital. As far as income situation is concerned, an investor with adequate income for normal needs from a salary, profession, business, or any other source can be more venturesome than an investor dependent on investments for all or a major part of his or her income. As for cash needs, an investor who knows that a significant amount of capital will be needed within a few years for the purchase of a home or a business, or for an extended foreign trip or any other purpose, could see that as a reason for being more conservative than would otherwise be the case. The time when those funds are required could coincide with a downswing in market cycles in common stocks or property. This could justify a decision to commit a smaller proportion of funds to that area than would otherwise be suitable.

A policy for an individual would naturally change over a number of years. In the few years immediately before retirement, investors could see merit in gradually phasing into the more defensive investment that is appropriate in retirement years. An investor whose family commitments have declined because children have become self-supporting may be able to adopt a more venturesome policy than would have been appropriate previously. Changed circumstances resulting in an increase in income from other sources could justify a more venturesome policy. Reduction or elimination of income from other sources could justify a more defensive policy.

Investment Strategy

Once an investment policy is settled, there then remain decisions on the strategy for putting that policy into effect in the face of current investment realities. Sometimes investment realities could justify a decision to modify, or perhaps suspend for the time being, the basic investment policy.

For example, a person with an adequate income from other sources and no major cash needs could make a policy decision that a reasonable proportion of his funds could be placed in medium risk investments such as common stocks, income producing property, and the like (while leaving some funds in lower risk investments as a "sheet anchor" for protection against sudden, unanticipated declines in markets). But an assessment of current market conditions may show that the market is vulnerable to decline because prices of equities relative to other investments are very high, or because interest rates are likely to rise and economic conditions to turn unfavorable. In that event, the appropriate strategy for that person would be to defer at least part of his or her planned equity investments until they were available at more realistic prices. In the meantime, the investor could "keep his powder dry" by placing the funds in short- to medium-term investments such as money market funds, short-term bonds, etc.

Investment Management

Investments do not look after themselves. Circumstances can change both in relation to the investments and the conditions of the investor. Hence, investments should be under constant review. This involves not only review of investment policy and strategy, but a review of the prospects of the particular investment, any changes in the safety ranking of fixed interest investments, and other considerations discussed later in this book.

For the investor who is managing his or her own investments, it is important to remember these points. For the person who decides to use specialist investment management through mutual funds or delegation of the management task to investment specialists, there is a need to review the performance record, attitude, and philosophies of those relevant investment managers.

The Importance of the Portfolio Effect

One of the most common mistakes made by investors is to make investment decisions without considering the impact of those decisions on the overall portfolio. It is the effect of a decision on the overall portfolio which really matters. This question must be considered in every investment decision. In the case of the portfolio in which the present portion funds in medium risk investments are well below what is appropriate from the viewpoint of investment policy and strategy, as discussed above, an addition to the portfolio of another medium risk investment would be reasonable. But for a portfolio with a proportion in that category which is already excessive, such an investment (even an investment which in its own right looks attractive) could be most unwise. If the investment is so attractive that there is a strong case for its inclusion in the latter portfolio, a place should be found for it by selling one or more of the other investments in that category. This could ensure that the portfolio remains properly balanced with the investments in that category not exceeding the planned percentage of the total portfolio.

part 2

The First R—
Return on Investments

4

Some Basic (but Not Well-Understood) Facts about Return

"I don't want a return *on* my investment," quipped comedian Eddie Cantor during the depression of the 30s, "—all I want is a return *of* my capital." In conditions more favorable than the depths of the Great Depression, most investors would like to get a return *on* their capital as well as a return *of* their capital when the investment is sold or matures. The facts are that many investors have a fairly vague, imprecise notion of many basic facts in thinking about a return on investments.

How Good Is Good?

Some investments are made because investors are given many reasons for that investment being "a good investment." Often they are not told precisely how good it is. If it is an equity investment, is it likely to produce a return (including income and capital gain components) sufficiently high to justify the greater risk involved in that type of investment? That and other questions are often not considered. Often an investment is made on the basis of a recommendation based on general statements, including many of the fallacies which were discussed in Chapter 2. Only a rational, somewhat critical approach to the question can produce the answers which are needed for sound decisions.

The Two Basic Elements in Investment Return

The two basic elements in return on any investment are:

1. Income return.
2. Capital gain or loss.

The overall return on an investment is the income return plus the capital gain or minus the capital loss after taking into account costs associated with investments such as brokerage, commission, and legal expenses. A good deal of talk about equity investments such as stocks or real estate refers to capital gain as though it were absolutely assured, but makes little or no reference to capital loss. The facts are that every single investment which *may provide capital gain inevitably carries with it the possibility of capital loss* (except where there is some special arrangement under which the investor is given a satisfactory guarantee against capital loss).

For common stock investments and preference stock, the income return is the dividend usually paid quarterly. On property investments, the income is the excess of rents received in a period over the expenses such as property taxes, insurance, repairs, maintenance, and depreciation. In direct business investments, the income is the net profit earned by the business.

Capital gain or capital loss is the difference between the amount received on the sale of an investment such as common stocks, property, or commodities and the cost price after allowing for buying and selling costs.

Is the Return Stable, Variable, Volatile?

With loan investments such as bonds (often referred to as fixed interest investment), the borrower (government or corporation) has an obligation to pay the agreed rate of interest. That type of income can be regarded as fairly assured. Interest has to be paid by a corporation whether or not it makes a profit in a particular year. Only the serious financial problems of a company could prevent it from paying interest. But even in those circumstances, investors usually enjoy some priority in payment which puts them in a stronger position than common stockholders. Provided reasonable steps are taken to assess the safety ranking of the companies or governments issuing the loan, income of that type could be considered fairly assured.

Dividends, by contrast, are not assured and have to be considered as variable. They can vary because of variations in the earnings of the company and also because of decisions by the board as to what portion of earnings is to be paid out as dividends and what portion is to be retained by the company. As most companies pay out only a portion of available profits in dividends, there is some stability, as a significant reduction in earnings per share may not necessarily mean any reduction or a fully proportionate reduction in dividend payments. In portfolios in which equity funds are spread over a number of different stocks, the stability is increased, as any decline in payments by one company may be offset by increased dividend payments by another.

The volatile element of return on equity investments is the capital gain or loss component. Due to cyclical swings and, in recent years, extremely increased speculation (even by institutions trying to outperform each other in the short term), movements can become very volatile. This factor, which traditional investment wisdom has tended to disregard, is a key element in investment decisions today.

Actual Money and Maybe Money

It is very important to remember the difference between actual money and maybe money. Actual money is income earned, for example, interest on fixed interest investments. For the reasons outlined above, a fairly well-spread stock portfolio could consider the income return as being in the actual money category, though there could be some variation. On income-producing property, net income could also be considered as actual money, although there may be some variation due to such factors as changes in revenue lost through increased vacancies, or increase in cost not covered by increased rent.

Maybe money is primarily the capital gain that is achieved if all goes well. For investors in stocks, the retained earnings, that is, the portion of earnings that is not paid out in dividends but is retained by the company, is also maybe money. The extent to which an investor benefits from retained earnings depends on market cycles and other factors, which are discussed later.

In terms of outlays, the cost of a property project is actual money, but the sale proceeds that are estimated are maybe money. Interest on borrowed funds is actual money. Additional capital gain which may be expected through the leverage or multiplying effect using borrowed funds is very much in the category of maybe money. Deciding whether to sell investments such as property at present or to expend further capital in borrowing or extending in the hope of increasing both its earning capacity and capital value, the expenditure is actual money and the other two items maybe money.

5

Time Value of Money, Compounding, and Allied Topics

In recent times, investors who thought they had done very well out of real estate investments which doubled in value in five or six years tended to ignore the significance of the time value of money and compounding. If a block of land doubles in value in a period of six years, it has increased at a rate of about 12 percent per annum compound. That figure would have to be reduced first to allow for buying and selling costs, which may have worked out at the equivalent of 1 percent per annum. Property taxes and other costs may have amounted to about 3 percent per annum. In that event, the investment which did not produce any income because it was vacant would have earned about 8 percent per annum. But bond investors were then earning between 10 and 15 percent per annum, depending on when they made their investments. Even after allowing for tax benefit if the capital gain was lower than the income tax payable by the bond investor, the bond tortoise may well have outpaced the real estate hare in this contest.

Present Value and Compound Sum

A person prepared to sell something for $1,000 cash would insist on a larger payment if the whole of the amount were to be paid one, two, or three years later. If money can earn 10 percent per annum, then $1,000 cash invested at 10 percent would grow to $1,100 in one year. In two years it would be worth $1,210 (in the second year the accumulated principal of $1,100 at 10 percent would earn $110 in interest). By the end of the third year it would be worth $1,331.

Thus the seller, on the basis of a 10 percent interest rate, would require a payment of $1,100 at the end of one year, $1,210 at the end of two years, and $1,331 at the end of three years. The latter figures are the amount to which $1,000 invested at 10 percent would grow in one, two, and three years. To look at it from the other point of view, the present value of a compound sum of $1,100 in one year, $1,210 in two years, or $1,331 in three years, with interest rates at 10 percent, is $1,000.

Present Value in Investment Decisions

Business management, in considering the relative merits of different machinery providing different cash flow figures, use the present value approach. They calculate the present value of future cash flows (both cash flowing out on the purchase of the equipment and cash flowing in from revenue or savings it produces) for the various periods. A portfolio investor can use the present value concept as the basis of arriving at a price to be paid for the purchase of a bond in the market. If the bond is paying interest at a rate exactly equal to the going rate in the market, then its value would be its face value plus any accrued interest since the date of the last periodical interest payment. If the interest rate it is paying is higher than the going market rate, then the bond will have a value above its face value or the figure at which it will be redeemed. On the other hand, if the interest rate it is paying is lower than the going market rate, then its market value would be at a discount below the face value.

Calculation of the Value of a Bond

To calculate the value of a bond in current market conditions, there are two elements to be calculated:

1. Present value of the face value amount of the bond to be received on maturity.
2. The present value of the stream of interest payments to be received from date of purchase to maturity or redemption date of the bond.

Let us take an example of a bond with a face value of $1,000 on which the "coupon" interest, that is, the interest rate payable on the bond in terms of the conditions of issue, is 8 percent per annum. The market yield, that is, the yield obtainable on purchase of bonds of that type, is 11 percent per annum, and the bond has three years to maturity. As it is paid half-yearly, we convert the coupon interest rate, the market yield, and the periods to maturity to the equivalent half-year figures, namely, coupon interest rate of 4 percent per half year, market yield of 5.5 percent per half year, and periods to maturity as six half years.

The first element in the present value of the bond is calculated as follows:

$$PV = FV (1 + i)^{-n}$$

where PV equals present value, F equals face value, i equals the interest rate per period to maturity, and n equals the number of periods to maturity.

From the figures given above, the calculations are as follows:

$$
\begin{aligned}
PV &= FV (1 + i)^{-n} \\
&= 1{,}000 \times (1.055)^{-6} \\
&= 1{,}000 \times (0.72525) \\
&= \$725.25
\end{aligned}
$$

Turning to the second element, the formula for the present value of a payment of $1 per period is as follows:

$$
\begin{aligned}
PV &= \frac{1 - (1 + i)^{-n}}{i} \\
&= \frac{1 - (1.055)^{-6}}{.055} \\
&= \frac{1 - 0.72525}{.055} \\
&= \$4.995
\end{aligned}
$$

As that is the present value of $1 per period and the $1,000 bond paying 8 percent per annum equal to 4 percent per half year would pay $40 per period, the present value of that payment equals $40 \times 4.995 = \$199.80$. Hence, the present value of the bond is the sum of the two elements calculated above, $725.25 plus $199.80, which equals $925.05. The overall formula for the value of the bond, including the two elements above, can be written as follows:

$$PV = [FV (1 + i)^{-n}] + \left[FV \times R \left(\frac{1 - (1 + i)^{-n}}{i}\right)\right]$$

Where PV is the overall present value of the bond, the other items have the same meaning as above and R is the coupon rate, or the rate of interest per period. In the above calculations, the coupon interest rate and market yield, which are normally expressed as percentages, are converted to their decimal equivalents, for example, 5.5 percent $= .055$ and 4 percent $= .04$.

Amount to Pay Off Mortgage Debts

The second element in the formula for calculation of bonds discussed above is also used in calculating the amount which would be required to pay off a mortgage. That calculation involves arriving at the present value of future monthly installments. Suppose a mortgage had been arranged at 12 percent per annum, equal to 1 percent per month, and six years of the original term are still to go; that is, there are 72 further monthly installments of $180. The amount required to pay off that mortgage can be calculated as follows:

$$PV = 180 \times \left[\frac{1 - (1.01)^{-72}}{.01}\right]$$
$$= 180 \times 51.1504$$
$$= 9,207$$

Compound Rates of Growth

From the figures quoted in the early paragraphs of this chapter, the difference between simple interest and compound interest can be appreciated. If $1,000 is invested at 10 percent and the interest is paid over each year, then in the third year and, indeed, all subsequent years the interest payment on an investment of $1,000 would be $100. But where the interest is not paid over in the third year, it is not $100 but $121, because the capital in the beginning of that year, including the accumulated interest, has grown from $1,000 to $1,210.

For any figures involving growth, it is necessary to express them in terms of compound rates per cent per annum. This applies to growth of population as well as to growth in investments and financial matters. It is important to remember this point, because some sales people trying to create a favorable picture of certain types of investment are inclined to ignore this fact. In referring to a particular type of investment in which the capital value has grown from $1,000 to $4,000 over 15 years, a salesperson may claim that it represents a growth rate of 20 percent per annum ($4,000 minus $1,000 equals $3,000, which is 300 percent of the original capital. Divide by 15 and you have an alleged annual growth rate of 20 percent per annum.) In fact, the investment has grown at a compound rate of 9.7 percent per annum. That figure, which correctly reflects the rate of growth, is vastly different from the incorrect figure arrived at by those who ignore the need to calculate in terms of compound rate of growth.

The Significance of Compounding

At 10 percent per annum, an amount will double in about seven years. In 30 years it would grow to over 17 times the original amount. At larger interest rates or rates of growth, it become even more significant. If an investment could maintain a rate of growth of 30 percent per annum (as we shall see below, this is highly unlikely), in 25 years it would grow to no less than 706 times its original size.

There is the story that the late Lord Keynes illustrated the importance of compounding by referring to the value of one of the ships and cargo captured by the English raider Drake. He stated that the value of one of those ships 400 years ago compounded at 4 percent per annum compound would have grown by the 30s of this century to a figure equal to the value of all British overseas investments at that time.

Why High Growth Rates Cannot Be Sustained

If you or your parents or grandparents purchased shares at the low point of the Great Depression of 1932 and sold at the record high level in 1933, what rate of capital growth would have been achieved? Would it have been 20 percent, 50 percent, or 100 percent? It would have been none of those figures, but in fact a modest rate of 6.9 percent per annum compound. Sales people or others making a superficial assessment who ignore the need to calculate in terms of compound rate of growth would claim a growth rate of about 58 percent per annum. In realistic terms of compound growth, it works out at 6.9 percent per annum compound from 41 to 1,233 in 50.8 years.

One significant point in investments which should never be forgotten is that few, if any, investments are able to maintain growth rates above 10 to 15 percent per annum in the long term. They may do so for 2 or 3 years or perhaps a few more years, but for periods of 5 to 10 years or longer, high rates of growth are not maintained. Those who claim that certain investments have maintained very high rates of growth are making comments based on wishful thinking rather than realities. Recall the point made above that if the investment were to grow at 30 percent per annum, it would in 25 years reach a figure 706 times the original figure. This would mean that if that rate of growth had been maintained in the past, a property now worth over $700,000 would have been worth only $1,000 25 years ago. There would be few, if any, cases where that situation would represent the facts.

This fact of life is very significant in investment decisions. It means that you should not make any investment decisions on the expectation that high rates of growth will be maintained. If an investment has maintained a high growth rate for a number of years, it could be vulnerable to decline. Experience would suggest that sooner or later, and perhaps sooner rather than later, there could be a reaction which could pull prices down to the path representing a more sustainable rate of growth.

Another point that has to be considered is that because of the power of compounding, there can be all sorts of physical constraints on the ability of the investments to grow. Years ago, a cynic pointed out that many of the optimistic estimates of the growth of earnings of IBM would in about 20 years have given it earnings figures which would exceed the gross domestic product at that time of the whole U.S. economy.

If high rates of growth in values of city buildings and rents for those buildings were to be maintained for 20 or 30 years, it could be shown that rental payments alone would absorb the whole or almost the whole of the estimated gross domestic product at that time—with nothing left for food, clothing, transportation, and all the other goods and services in the economy.

A Rule of Thumb for Compounding Calculations

There is a rule of thumb in relation to compounding which is helpful in giving a quick "ball park" answer. This rule is as follows:

1. If you divide the interest rate into 72, the answer is the approximate number of periods it would take for an amount to double at that interest rate. For example, at 10 percent interest it would double in a little over seven years, at 12 percent in about six years, and at 15 percent in about five years.
2. The number of years grows by arithmetic progression, and the approximate figure to which the amount would have grown increases by geometric progression. For example, we saw above that at 12 percent interest an amount will double in about six years. In a further 6 years, a total of 12, it would have grown to about 4 times the original size, in 18 years to 8 times the original size, and in 24 years to about 16 times the original figure.

Compound Calculations

In some relatively inexpensive calculators, it is possible to use exponents, that is, to raise a figure to a certain power. For example, these machines could calculate the amount to which a figure should grow in four years at 12 percent per annum (i.e., calculate 1.12 raised to the fourth power). It is generally done by keying in the figure of 1.12, then a key for raising of the exponents, and then keying in the exponent (i.e., 4). The calculator would then display the answer 1.5735.

If you wanted to calculate $(1.12)^{-4}$, you would do the calculations as above and then press the 1/x key to get the reciprocal of that figure. If there is no reciprocal key, it would be obtained by dividing one by the figure as calculated above. If such a machine is not available, there are financial tables that show amounts in present value, which have been discussed in this chapter. If they are not available but you have access to a table of logarithms, these can be used to raise a figure to a power by the use of the logarithm of that figure for the power to which you wish to raise it. For example, to raise 1.12 to the fourth power, first determine from logarithm tables the logarithm for 1.12, which is 0.04922. Multiply that figure by 4, which gives you 0.19688. Then from the table of anti-logarithms determine the answer, which is 1.574.

Calculation of Growth Rates

The rate at which investments have grown over a period can be calculated from this formula:

$$G = \left[\sqrt[n]{\frac{V2}{V1}} - 1 \right] \times 100$$

G equals the compound rate of growth expressed as a percentage, n equals the number of periods, $V2$ equals the value of the investment at the end of a period, and $V1$ equals the value of the investment at the beginning of the period. In fact, this formula calculates the nth root of the ratio of the closing value to the opening value and subtracts 1 from that value to get the rate of growth as a decimal. Multiplying that figure by 100 expresses it as a percentage.

For example, if an investment has grown from $1,000 to $3,000 in 10 years, the compound rate of growth is calculated as follows:

$$G = \left[\sqrt[10]{\frac{3,000}{1,000}} - 1 \right] \times 100$$

$$= [\sqrt[10]{3} - 1] \times 100$$
$$= [1.116 - 1] \times 100$$
$$= 11.6\% \text{ per annum compound rate of growth}$$

6

Income—the First Component of Investment Return

When the March Hare in *Alice in Wonderland* told Alice that she should say what she means, she replied, "I do, at least—at least I mean what I say—that's the same thing, you know." We chuckle at Alice's comment, which suggests that the words she uses mean exactly what she wants them to mean. But we all have a tendency to preconceived notions of what particular words mean, which may sometimes be unrealistic. So it is worthwhile to consider briefly what the nature of income is from the viewpoint of an investor.

An economist regards as income the amount which could be expended (or distributed to shareholders or others) without reducing the capital of the entity. Hence, it would include not only income in the accounting sense of the word, which is the excess of periodic income over periodic costs, but also any increase or decrease in the capital value of assets.

Investment return, that is, the overall result of an investment, is comprised of income plus capital gain or minus capital loss arising from the change in value of the assets. But in looking at the components of investment return, it is income in the accounting sense of the term which is relevant.

Fixed Income and Variable Income

Loan investments such as bonds, mortgages, and deposits with banks or other institutions provide a fixed rate of investment income. There is a contractual obligation for the interest to be paid regardless of the rate of profits or losses earned by the organization to which the money is lent. These investments are often referred to as fixed interest investments.

For equity investments which involve ownership or part ownership of a business (such as common stock, real estate, or direct investment in a business), the income is variable. It can vary depending on the profits earned by the relevant business or the liquid cash position of the company. It can also be affected by policy decisions of the board of the company as to what part, if any, of available profits is to be distributed as dividends and what part is to be retained in the business.

The income received by individual investors can vary because of the different prices at which the investments were purchased. Consider two investors holding the same amount of stock in a company, with Investor A having bought his shares at a time when the market was low for a price just half that paid later by Investor B. Though they would both receive the same amount of dividend, the return to Investor A as a percentage of his capital investment would be twice the return earned by Investor B.

Arguments for and against Payment of No Dividend

Some companies pay no dividends at all, with the whole of the profits otherwise available for dividends being retained in the business to finance expansion. An argument advanced in favor of this policy is that if the profits are distributed in whole or in part as dividends, the investors have to pay income tax on the dividend received. Then, if further funds are needed, the company has to approach the shareholders for capital, which in effect means that they then pay back part of the dividend received on which they have already paid tax. Another argument in favor of this course is that companies with good growth prospects should be able to use their financial strength, established organization, financial and marketing expertise in making better use of the funds of stockholders than the individual stockholders could.

Hence, it is better for the funds to be retained and for the investors to enjoy the benefit through the enhanced value of their shares and capital gain on which the tax burden would be lower (and it would not arise until the stock was sold).

The main argument against this course of action is that it is based on the fallacy that retained profits will be reflected in enhanced market value for the stock. The fact is that dividend receipts from the investor's viewpoint are actual money, while retained earnings are very much in the nature of maybe money. Whether and to what extent stockholders derive any benefit in enhanced market values through retained profits depends on a whole host of factors. These include market cycles, changes in market fashions, changes in interest rates and the relative costs of other investments, inflow and outflow of funds from institutions by foreign investors, as well as the future earnings experience of the company.

A further argument against the no dividend policy is that the stockholders include large numbers of individuals and institutions with different cash needs and taxation situations. Hence, it is preferable for stockholders to receive at least some dividends so that they can make their own decision on what they wish to do with them.

Perhaps an even more telling argument against the no dividend policy is the fact that, in general, the lower the income component of the overall investment return, the greater is the risk involved. If there is no dividend payment, the whole of the expected return has to come from the more volatile area of the maybe money of the capital gain. This tends to increase the downside risk of adverse market movements. Experience shows that low-yielding or no-yielding investments that may improve in value greatly in favorable times, often decline more rapidly when the market tide turns.

The Crucial Effect of Market Price at Time of Purchase

The point has already been made that the investor who was wise enough or fortunate enough to purchase an investment at a time when market values were low derives a higher return on his investment than would be earned by those who bought at higher prices. In an equity investment such as common stocks and real estate, where markets tend to follow a more or less wavelike cyclical pattern, the timing of purchase can often have a more significant effect on the rate of return on the investment as far as income is concerned than other factors such as selection of stocks. (Generally the same factor would also be significant in relation to the other component of investment return, capital gain, as well.)

Though this influence is more marked in relation to equity investments such as common stocks and real estate, it may also have a bearing on the return from loan or fixed interest investment. For example, those who invested in this area at times of high interest rates such as 1981–82 would now be enjoying a relatively high return. That return would be higher either because they subscribed for new investments at the higher rates than ruling, or because they purchased in the market stock issued earlier at low interest rates at a discount below face value to provide a return about equal to the higher return available at that time on newly issued stock.

Range of Income on Bonds and Other Loan Investments

The income return on loan investments such as bonds or mortgages is affected by a number of factors. One is the level of interest rates at the time of making the investment. Interest rates, in turn, are affected by factors such as variations in the supply of, and demand for, funds by governments and commercial borrowers, the level of inflation and expectations about trends in inflation figures, and to some extent by interest rate trends in other parts of the world.

In the second half of 1983, the U.S. medium- and long-term interest rates in real terms (i.e., the excess of interest rates above the inflation rate) were at very high levels. By contrast, 10 to 30 years earlier the real interest rates were low and at times negative, with the nominal interest rates being lower than the inflation rate. This change is due partly to greater attention given to money supply and recognition by governments that high interest rates may be inevitable in times of large government deficits, if the money supply is to be controlled to combat inflation.

In recent years, medium- and long-term interest rates have varied between about 9 percent and 13 percent for most of the time. Prior to the early 1970s, rates generally were lower, in the 3 to about 6 percent range.

Generally, short-term rates are lower than medium- and long-term rates. But these rates are volatile, and at times of tight money they can rise to very high levels, for example, the prime bank rate around 20 percent in the early 80s.

Range of Income on Common Stocks and Other Equities

On common stocks and other equities, the income range tends to be considerably greater. Though income return on these investments can vary depending on the success of the company in the case of common stock, revenue and expenditure on real estate or business investment, overall trends in the economy, and expectation about those factors, there is as well another crucial factor. It is the timing of the purchase of the investment. As well as the cyclical pattern of market movements resulting in higher yields on investment cost to those who buy when share prices are low near the bottom of a cycle, there is also the effect of longer term trends. Some 30 years ago, the average dividend yield was between 5.5 and 6 percent. About 15 years ago, in the mid-60s, enthusiasm for equity investments had pushed prices up to levels at which dividend yields were down to about 3.2 percent.

If the dividend yield is related to returns available from other investments such as bonds, the change is even more significant. In 1953, the average dividend yield of 5.9 percent was more than half as high again as the Aaa bond yield of 3.2 percent. About the middle of 1983, after the rise of about 50 percent in the stock market, the average dividend yield of just under 4 percent was well below half the bond yield at the time of about 11.5 percent.

Various Means of Measuring Investment Income

There are various means of measuring income yields which provide some sort of basis for comparison of stocks with different market values and different rates of dividend payment. One is the dividend yield, which is the dividend divided by the cost of the stock multiplied by 100 to express it as a percentage. That figure is the percentage return from the income component of the investment enjoyed by a particular investor in relation to his cost price. Another matter which is frequently quoted in the financial press relates to earnings. A similar calculation to that above using earnings, per share and divided by the cost of the shares gives the earnings yield. If this is expressed another way by dividing the price per share by the earnings per share, the result is the *price earnings multiple.* That is what investment people mean when they talk of a stock having a "p.e. of . . . ." Most investment analysts tend to use the price earnings multiple and earnings yield in discussing values of stocks, but this could be more a matter of tradition than logic, as the dividend yield, which they would regard as old-fashioned, is more significant. It is one of the two components of overall investment return. By contrast, the earnings yield, or that portion of it which is not received as dividend, is not a specific portion of investment return and in fact, as pointed out earlier, may not necessarily be reflected in the share prices.

For many purposes, a more important measure is what relates the income from an equity investment with income available elsewhere. This matter is discussed more fully in later chapters dealing with the concept of relative costs.

Use of Current Market Value Rather than Cost Price

In determining the dividend yield, earnings yield, or price earnings multiple on a stock which you are about to purchase, it is the cost price, or the market value at that time, which is relevant. Later, in calculating the yield of that and other investments on invested capital, it is the cost price, or the market value at the date of purchase, which is relevant for that purpose.

But for most investment decisions, the present and the future are more important than the past. So it may be necessary to consider the income component of overall return on the basis of the dividend yield based on current market price rather than on the cost price at some earlier date. The reason is that the opportunity cost (this term is discussed in later chapters) of continuing to hold that investment involves a consideration of the market value. If you bought the investment many years ago at a much lower price, it may be showing you a good yield in relation to your cost price. But if you continue to hold it and give up the opportunity of selling it at the current market value, it is the yield on the current market that is important. You have to consider whether that yield justifies continuing to hold that investment, compared with switching to other investments which offer either a better income return on the current market, better prospects of capital gain, or both.

Significance of Income for Various Investors

The income component of overall investment return is very important for some investors with limited capital, or for those depending on their investments for all or a major part of their normal income. It is a good deal less important to those with adequate income from other sources and large amounts of capital, who could afford to have at least some of their capital in investments producing a low income, no income, or even a negative income (for example, vacant land which produces no cash inflow and involves a cash outflow for payment of property taxes and other holding costs).

Taxation may also affect the relative attractions of the income component of overall investment return to various investors. Those who are in a high personal tax bracket may see some merit in placing more of their funds in low income yielding investments with prospects of capital gain than people in the lower income tax bracket or investors not subject to tax.

Investors Seeking Capital Growth Also Need to Consider Income

Some investors may not have the income component of overall return as a major priority. Because of adequate cash, or because they are in a high income tax bracket, it may suit them to plan their investments in such a way that the bulk of their return comes from capital gain, on which capital gains tax would be lower than tax on income. At first sight, it may appear that these investors would have little or no interest in the income earned by an investor.

Further consideration shows that the income situation is of some importance even to those investors. The reason is that the income earned by an investment is relevant in such questions as the cost of an investment relative to other investments (which is discussed in several later chapters), or as a general indicator of whether investments may be reaching the stage where they are vulnerable to severe downside risk. These questions are discussed more fully in later chapters.

7

Capital Gain or Loss— the Second Element in Investment Return

The income component of investment return discussed in the last chapter could be described as the actual money component. (Income return on many investments is not guaranteed and may vary, but with careful selection and a spread over different risk categories income tends to be fairly stable with relatively low downside risk.) In this chapter we turn to the second component of *capital gain* through an increase in the market value of the investment, or *capital loss* through a decline in that market value (in both cases, after allowing for the transaction costs of buying and selling the investment), which we can call the maybe money component.

The uncertainty and, to some extent, the difficulty of predicting capital gain or loss need to be stressed. Otherwise, investors may be misled by the comments of sales people and enthusiastic supporters of some equity investments, which suggest that capital gain is absolutely assured and there is little or no prospect of capital loss. The facts are different. Any investment that offers prospects for capital gain inevitably carries with it the possibility of capital loss through a decline in market values. There is no investment that provides automatic or assured capital gain. Another point worth remembering is that even when capital gain is achieved, it may not be readily available until an investment is sold. The unrealized capital gain cannot be used to buy food or clothes, or to pay bills. Even the most sophisticated electronic equipment at the supermarket check-out cannot accept unrealized capital gain in payment for goods purchased.

Some disappointed investors who have not achieved the capital gain which they were led to believe an investment would produce, come to regard capital gain as a will-o'-the-wisp—here today, gone tomorrow. It is certainly true that rising market prices do not continue forever. Often

market booms end and are succeeded by serious slumps, often when least
expected by many people in the marketplace.

The Many Faces of Capital Gain or Loss

Capital gain can arise in many ways and from many different sources.
Before going into these more specifically, a few general observations may
be of interest. Sometimes capital gain is the recognition by the market of
good results or good prospects of a company because of astute marketing,
sound investment decisions or wise acquisitions of other companies,
innovations in developing a new product (for example, the Apple Computer Company in its early years), or improved management, cost reduction, or other efficiency improvement.

Sometimes capital gain in the short term may represent little more than
increased prices because the particular investment is "flavor of the
month." Local and overseas personal and institutional investors may be
pushing market values higher and higher as they outbid each other in a
frenzy of enthusiasm. On the other hand, after a market has been depressed for a long time, capital gain can arise primarily through recovery
from excessive pessimism of the past.

Capital loss can arise pretty much from the converse of the factors
outlined above. Both capital gain and capital loss can be affected by all
sorts of factors, which are discussed in this and later chapters.

Gain in "Ordinary Investments," Loss in "Good Investments"

"Good investments" can, in fact, turn out to be very poor investments.
More correctly, investments which are described as good (for example,
stock in well-known companies), can be poor investments for the person
who purchases them just before a market decline. An example is the
decline of over 80 percent in the market value of Avon Product shares
between 1972 and 1974, partly due to an overall market decline and
partly in reaction to the excessive rises of earlier years.

On the other hand, good capital gain can be achieved in far less
prestigious investments which are bought and sold at the right time.
Some experienced investors say there is no such thing as a good investment or a bad investment, simply some investments which are likely to go
up and some which are likely to go down.

The Two Basic Sources of Capital Gain or Loss

There are many different reasons for particular investments at particular
times producing capital gain or loss. But all of those reasons could

generally be classified under one or the other of two basic sources of change in market values. It is well to note these two basic sources as a help in understanding the nature of capital gain and loss. The basic sources of capital gain or loss are as follows:

1. A change in capital value reflecting changes in the earning capacity of the investment.
2. Changes in capital values reflecting changes in the capitalization rate applied by the market (the ratio of market value to earnings from time to time).

The essential relationship can be seen from the following formula for calculating the price of an equity investment:

$$P = E \times 100/C$$

where P is price of an equity investment, E is net earnings of the investment, and C is the capitalization rate expressed as a percentage.

Let us assume that a particular investment is earning $1,000 per annum and the market capitalization rate is 12.5 percent. In that event, the investment would sell at $8,000 ($1,000 × 100 ÷ 12.5). If the investment, because of better conditions, better management, or whatever, increased its earnings from $1,000 to $1,500 and the market sentiment and capitalization rate were unchanged, then the price of the investment would increase to $12,000 ($1,500 × 100 ÷ 12.5). The increase of 50 percent in earnings is reflected by an increase of 50 percent in capital value. Let us now assume that earnings remained unchanged but the market capitalization rate changed. This could be due to all sorts of factors which are discussed later, including changes in interest rates and the returns available from other investments, economic trends, and the degree of confidence or pessimism in the market. If, due to any one or more of those causes, the market reached the view that instead of a capitalization percentage of 12.5 percent, 10 percent would be an appropriate rate, then the capital value of the investment which is earning $1,000 per annum would be $10,000. ($1,000 × 100 ÷ 10). So capital value is increased by 25 percent ($2,000 on $8,000) because the market is now working on a lower capitalization percentage. (Because of the inverse relationship, the lower the capitalization percentage or earnings yield, as it is sometimes called, the higher the market price and vice versa.)

There can be combinations of both of those factors in the change in market value over a period. An increase in capital value due to increased earnings may be augmented by a further increase due to a lower capitalization rate—possibly because of a greater recognition of the qualities and prospects of the investment which has produced the increased earnings.

Naturally, a decline in earnings or an increase in the capitalization percentage or earnings yield figure can work in the opposite direction.

It is well to remember this basic, simple relationship in considering scope for possible increase in capital value of an investment which you are considering. You could, for example, be more confident if there seemed to be ample scope for either an increase in earnings or an increase in capitalization rate than if either or both of those factors have little or no scope for improvement.

8

Possible Sources of Capital Gain or Loss

An investment specialist claimed that he was not a person to give indefinite answers as to how the stock market would perform, or to qualify his answers with all sorts of "ifs" and "buts." He said he would give a clear, unequivocal, one-word answer to the question as to what the market would do, and that answer was fluctuate. Certainly stock markets and, to a lesser extent, other investment markets do fluctuate a good deal. Sometimes they increase or decrease by a large amount in a short period. Periods when it seems the market is predetermined to move ever and ever upward are followed by periods of significant decline. At other times, the market moves up a little and down a little and really moves nowhere for a considerable period, with little or no net gain or loss. Before going on to consider the specific sources of capital gain or loss, it would be well to consider the range of these capital gains or losses.

Possible Range of Gains or Losses

In the nine months between the end of July 1982 and April 1983, the U.S. stock market, as measured by the Dow Jones Industrial Index, increased by 52 percent. That rise over nine months is equivalent to an annual rate of increase of 69 percent. In the next seven months, up to the end of November 1983, the index rose by only about 4 percent. That increase, which would be barely sufficient to cover buying and selling costs, works out at an annual rate of less than 8 percent—less than one eighth of the rate of increase from July 1982 to April 1983.

Over longer periods, there are significant differences in market behavior. In general, the 1950s and the early- and mid-60s were favorable with a good upward trend, subject to some cyclical downturns from time to time. From about 1967 to 1982, the tide tended to stay out for stock investors. Certainly there were gains for those who bought at low prices and sold at high points on the intermediate swings of two to three years, but the longer term trend was unfavorable. Indeed, the investor who purchased stocks at the high point around 1967 and had to sell or ran out of patience at mid-1982 could have incurred a loss of about 20 percent (in contrast to the gain of over 50 percent for the person who purchased in August 1982 and sold six or seven months later).

Other markets also have fluctuations. The stock market tends to be more volatile than real estate markets, partly because their movements are so widely publicized and sales can be made more readily. The basic point to note is that despite a lot of folklore and fallacies about investments, stocks, including stock of some of the best-known and most highly regarded companies, are subject to considerable fluctuation. This can mean the difference between a good capital gain and serious capital loss, depending on the timing of purchases and sales. In some investments such as futures trading, or equity investments such as real estate involving a significant amount of borrowing, losses can exceed the amount of the original investment.

Objective and Subjective Assessment—Actual and Perceived Information

In discussing possible sources of capital gain and loss, it is necessary to refer to estimates, assessments, or expectations about trends in the economy, in particular industries, or in the earnings of a particular company or a particular real estate investment. Those estimates involve information at two levels. First of all, there is what could be called the objective information—the information or estimates that could be made on a completely factual basis without much element of opinion being involved. The second element, which can often be more important in its impact on markets, is the subjective level—the level at which people make assessments involving not only the objective assessment but their interpretation of those trends and their assessments, based in part on their perception of the information or trends.

When markets are booming, there is a tendency for perceptions and expectations to be very optimistic. Investment analysts, even in attempting to make objective assessments, tend to look at figures and trends through somewhat rose-tinted glasses. *The longer the boom lasts, the greater is the rose tinting, so the figures tend to be distorted by a sort of exponential rose tinting.*

On the other hand, at times of market decline when an air of pessimism tends to pervade investment circles, the subjective estimates may be more pessimistic than would be objectively justified. In boom times, good news tends to be exaggerated in its effect and the bad news tends to be minimized or disregarded. The reverse applies in market slumps.

A good example is the fluctuations in the price of gold. In 1979, when gold prices were moving up very sharply, it was said by many people that any international problems would result in an increase in the price of gold. For a while this seemed to be the case, as any signs of increased international tension generally led to a further rise in the price of gold. Three years later when all sorts of international tensions were worsening, with problems in Afghanistan, Poland, Central America, and Lebanon, the gold price did not rise as news of new tensions developed. Increased tension, which a few years earlier would have been considered justification for a significant increase in the price of gold, had little or no effect on that price in the period of disenchantment when investors had seen that gold was not immune to the laws of gravity.

Changes Due to Basic Economics

In the last chapter we saw that one of the basic sources of capital gain or loss was reflection in market value of increases or decreases in the earnings of an equity investment. More specifically, increased earnings in a business, or prospects of better earnings in a business, better conditions in the industry, or better trends in the economy, could be the source of an increase in market value and hence capital gain on that investment.

If the capitalization rate was unchanged, then the capital gain would be proportional to the actual or expected improvement in those factors. If the air of confidence engendered by expectations of improvement led to the market being prepared to accept a lower earnings return and hence a higher price, then the increase in value due to the actual or expected improvement would be augmented by the higher market rating. On the other hand, actual or expected declines in earnings and industrial conditions or in overall economic trends could have the opposite effect.

Changes in interest rates, or in the returns available from other investments, may also have a significant effect on loan or fixed interest investments such as bonds or mortgages. Changes in interest rates have a direct, or more or less automatic, effect on capital value. Suppose a bond was issued two years ago at 10 percent per annum interest. Suppose the same bonds with exactly the same security and credit rating are now issued at 12 percent because of a general rise in interest rates in the economy. That rise in interest rates on new securities would reduce the value of the security issued earlier at a lower interest rate. The market value would be reduced because a buyer would obviously offer a price somewhat below face value for an investment paying 10 percent per annum when he or she has the option of subscribing for new issues at 12 percent per annum. There is an inverse relationship between changes in interest rates and capital value of previously issued stock—a rise in interest rates means a decline in capital value, and a decline in interest rates means a rise in capital value.

On equity investments such as shares or real estate, there is not the direct or automatic effect of a change in interest rates. But there could be some effect and should be some effect if markets were not distorted by other factors such as changes in expectations, market cycles, and the like. If interest rates rise and higher returns are now available on the loan or fixed interest investments, then if all other things were equal the equity market would also expect a higher return for a good investment, which would lead to a reduction in the market value. It doesn't always work out that way, because other factors could offset the impact of changing interest rates.

Changes in the attractions of other investments due to factors other than interest rates—for example, greater popularity, taxation, or other legislative concessions—may also have a spill-over effect on investment markets and hence the capital gain or loss achieved by investors.

Changes Associated with Investment Markets

In addition to the reflection in investment markets of the economic factors referred to above, there are a number of other effects which are more specifically associated with the markets themselves. The most important of these are:

1. Cycle. There is a tendency for most markets to move in a more or less wavelike cyclical pattern with significant declines from peak to trough, which could add to or offset the impact of economic and other factors.
2. Popularity and disenchantment. On the principle that nothing succeeds like success, markets that have been performing well with increase in values may for a period create their own momentum in which the effect of good news is accentuated and bad news is minimized. On the other hand, when markets have produced losses rather than gains for some time in the past, the disenchantment with that type of investment may offset or, indeed, overwhelm other favorable factors.
3. Fallacies and effective selling. Fallacies such as those discussed in an earlier chapter or effective selling, perhaps aided by higher commissions in one particular area, may make one class of invest-

ment considerably more favorable than others, and considerably more popular with buyers than would be justified on more objective grounds.

4. "The flavor of the month." Partly because of fallacies, partly because of the impact of persuasive sales people, and partly because of changing fashions in investments, as in other aspects of human activity, some markets or segments of markets may temporarily enjoy great popularity and sharp rises, for example, gambling stocks in the late 1970s, computer and high technology stocks in the early 80s.

Varying Impact on Equities and Fixed Interest Investments

Changes in capital value, and hence the capital gain or loss experience by investors, tends to be more significant for equity investors than for loan investors. That is not to say that loan investments, such as bonds and mortgages, cannot experience changes in value. Indeed, some investors who have gone into this type of investment to avoid capital loss may have been disappointed. If they invested in the early 70s at low interest rates in long-term bonds or mortgages, the subsequent sharp increase in interest rates on new investments of that type could have caused considerable capital loss to them.

But the point is that in the loan or fixed interest investments, steps can be taken to reduce the extent to which capital values are likely to fluctuate. This can be done partly by investing for relatively short periods of say three to four years, rather than for longer periods. (The shorter the period to maturity of these investments, the less is the impact on capital value of changes in interest rates on new securities.) Another is to concentrate on investments offering a better security or a higher safety ranking, and to spread investments with no more than about 10 to 15 percent invested in any one company or borrower.

If those steps are taken, the extent of capital fluctuation and the scope of capital gain and capital loss can be minimized. It is well to remember that in loan investments there is a contractual obligation for the borrower to repay the capital and to pay the interest as it falls due. In an equity investment such as purchase of stock or real estate, there is no such contractual obligation. Capital values in equity markets thus tend to fluctuate more significantly, partly because of business and financial uncertainties relating to that particular investment and partly because of factors such as market cycles and the other sources of capital gain and loss referred to above.

9

Impact of Taxation on Investment Returns

A sale, according to a facetious definition, is what some people go to to save more money than they can afford. In investments, some people get so carried away with the pursuit of tax benefits that they give insufficient attention to basic investment decisions. For them it is often the case of the taxation tail wagging the sound investment dog.

From time to time, news reports tell of large losses by celebrities in the entertainment and sporting world when some tax shelter scheme goes astray. Because of the bad management and sometimes the gross dishonesty of the promoters and managers of some of these tax schemes, the investors may lose both a considerable amount of capital and the tax benefits which they had hoped to achieve.

A Sane, Balanced Approach to Taxation and Investments

A sane, balanced approach to the question of taxation and investments should be on the following lines:

1. Be constantly aware of the significance of taxation and learn to think in terms of after-tax returns on investments.
2. Recognize the varying degree of risks in various methods of minimizing taxation, and don't expose your capital to an undue amount of risk.
3. Be sure to carefully check out the honesty, reliability, and financial soundness of the managers or promoters of investment schemes said to produce tax benefits.

As in so many areas, the prudent course is to aim for a happy medium between two extremes. You should avoid the extremes of, on the one hand, ignoring tax effects completely and, on the other hand, allowing tax considerations to distort the sound analysis and judgment that is needed in all investment decisions.

The Difference between Before- and After-Tax Returns

An investor needs to learn to apply the "bottom line" approach adopted by business people. This involves looking at the final result, which in the case of investment is the after-tax rate of return.

If you do not adopt this approach, you could make the mistake of selecting an investment with a higher before-tax return when another investment with a lower before-tax return would have been preferable because its after-tax return (the bottom line) is higher. For example, compare one investment providing a return of 12 percent per annum and no capital gain with another investment providing an income of 4 percent per annum and capital gain of 7 percent per annum, making a total of 11 percent. If we assume that the income tax rate is 40 percent (including federal and state) and the capital gains tax is 20 percent, the first investment produces an after-tax return of 7.2 percent (12 percent minus 40 percent of 12 percent, i.e., 4.8 percent).

On the other investment, the net income return after tax is 2.4 percent (4 percent minus 40 percent of 4 percent) and the net return on the capital gain component is 5.6 percent (7 percent minus 20 percent of 7 percent, i.e., 1.4 percent). So the total after-tax return on the second investment is 8 percent per annum (2.4 percent plus 5.6 percent), which is higher than the after-tax return of 7.2 percent per annum on the first investment, which had the higher before-tax return.

Capital gain can also provide a further advantage from the taxation point of view in that the payment of the tax is deferred. In the example above, in the interest of simplicity, calculations were made on the assumption that the capital gain of 7 percent per annum was received in part each year. Generally what happens is that the capital gain accumulates for perhaps many years and tax is paid only at the end of that period, when the investment is sold. In that event the effective cost of the tax is reduced, because the investors had the use of the money during that period.

This is an important point, especially in recent years when interest rates and hence the cost of money and returns available on investments have been much higher than in earlier years. Remember the old saying that "he gives twice who gives quickly." You can paraphrase this by saying "he pays less who pays later." When the time value of money is taken into account (including the fact that the money saved by not paying tax immediately could be invested or could reduce borrowings and save interest costs), the advantage in favor of the investment producing relatively low income and significant capital gain could be greater.

Hence, if all other things were equal, there would be a decided advantage, from a tax point of view, in going for investments which produced capital gain rather than income. But, as we shall see, all other things are not equal, and capital gain investments generally involve a greater degree of risk. Because markets are not a one-way street, the investments that can produce capital gain can also produce significant capital loss—the decline of about 70 percent in the price of Avon Products stock referred to in an earlier chapter is a reminder of this point.

Varying Degrees of Risk in Investments with Tax Benefits

Before going into any investment which appears to offer taxation benefits, it is important that you have a clear idea of the risks involved. Each investor has to decide whether the rewards in the investment, including the tax benefits, are reasonable in relation to the risks involved. You may also have to decide whether the degree of risk involved in the particular investment is more than you should be prepared to accept. An investor with limited capital and limited income may have to ignore investments with tax benefits, even if they involve relatively small risks. An investor with larger capital and a more adequate income from other sources could afford to take more risks, at least with part of his or her capital.

There is no way in which all of the various investments that may offer taxation benefits can be classified into any precisely determined degree of risk, because so much depends on the particular circumstances, the question of whether a particular market is high or low at the time of investment, and other factors. The following groupings of some types of investment which offer tax benefits could be useful in illustrating the range.

Low Risk Investments with Tax Benefits

Of the low risk investments which offer tax benefits, possibly the most attractive is the one which many people do not view primarily as an investment, that is, an investment in the purchase of their own home. There is a considerable tax benefit in the United States in investing capital in a home rather than in other assets. One reason is that the interest on borrowed funds used to finance the purchase is an allowable deduction for tax purposes. But the income earned by the investment—

the imputed income derived by the owner, which is the difference between the rent he or she would otherwise pay and the property taxes, insurance, etc., which he or she pays as owner—is not assessable income.

Another relatively low risk type of investment offering tax benefits is the use of borrowed funds, within prudent limits, to finance investments. The use of borrowed funds provides a leverage effect which can multiply the capital gain. For example, if you purchase a property which increases 25 percent in value and you financed it half from capital and half from borrowed funds, the capital gain on your outlay works out at 50 percent. If you had borrowed three quarters and financed only one quarter from your own capital, the 25 percent capital gain on the property would represent a gain of 100 percent on your investment. Naturally, you would have to allow for the interest cost.

If borrowing is kept within reason so that total liabilities do not exceed 50 percent of total assets and the cash flow, allowing for some possible reductions in adverse circumstances, is sufficient to meet interest payments and repayment of capital, the risk of borrowing can be kept to reasonable levels. The leverage through borrowing can work in two ways. As well as helping to produce a better overall effect, there is a further benefit on the after-tax income because the tax on capital gain is generally lower than the rate of tax payable on income. There is also the point made earlier in the chapter about the further benefit of deferring payment of capital gain tax for some years until the asset is sold.

Tax-free bonds of municipal organizations are another example of relatively low risk investments offering tax benefits.

The purchase of a business or a farm or other property which is run down may also be attractive in terms of taxation. If you are able to improve the income or the productive capacity of the business or property, you may be able to achieve significant capital gain, at relatively low tax rates. Some of the cost of achieving that increased earning capacity in terms of operational expenses, pastoral improvement, fertilizers, and repairs may also be fully deductible against current income in the year of expenditure. You would have to allow for normal business risk, including weather risk.

Medium Risk Investments with Tax Benefits

Among the medium risk investments which can offer tax benefits are what are described as tax shelter investments—investments that take advantage of provisions in the income tax legislation. One is investment in property involving the use of borrowed funds, as outlined above. Interest on borrowings may reduce the property net income to a loss figure which can be offset against other income.

In this category would also be grouped other tax shelters of various kinds which are managed by honest and competent managers, as distinct from the higher speculative tax shelters referred to below.

High Risk Investments with Tax Benefits

In this category would be the tax shelters involving a high degree of risk, such as investments in oil exploration, where the risks are necessarily greater than investing in a normal commercial venture.

A tax shelter managed by people who are inexperienced or dishonest, or both, is a very high risk operation. Indeed, in many of the tax shelter operations the biggest risk is associated with the question of the honesty and efficiency of the managers. In considering whether to go into any tax shelter scheme, this question should be given top priority in preliminary considerations. If there are any serious doubts on this score, it may well be wise to apply the principle: "If in doubt, stay out."

Outlaying Capital to Save Expenditure from After-Tax Income

It is a well-established principle of business that it is often wise to outlay capital on the purchase of equipment which will substantially reduce operating costs. From the viewpoint of an individual investor, taxation considerations can often make it worthwhile to consider outlaying capital in ways which will save expenditure from after-tax income—or, in other words, expenditure of a type which is not an allowable deduction for tax purposes. One simple example relates to a private automobile, for which running expenses are not deductible for tax purposes. Outlaying capital to replace a middle-aged automobile with a newer, more efficient vehicle may save a considerable amount because the newer car may be more fuel efficient. Moreover, repairs and maintenance will be a good deal lower on a new vehicle than on one which is several years old.

If the investor had retained the old automobile and invested elsewhere the capital that could have been expended on the purchase of a new vehicle, the investment income which he earns would be subject to tax (except to the extent to which he was able to offset it wholly or partly through tax benefits of the type described above). He then has to pay for his larger repair bills and perhaps higher fuel costs on the older vehicle out of his after-tax income. On the other hand, if he had outlaid the capital on the purchase of a new vehicle, the return he would derive from that expenditure is somewhat comparable to the income gained from investing in the purchase of a home, namely the savings of expenditure that otherwise would be involved. That "income" which in effect is earned through the savings of expenditure is not subject to taxation.

This does not, of course, mean that every purchase of a new automobile would be justified on these grounds. The taxation benefits would have to be weighed against all the other factors. Obviously, the benefit of outlaying capital in this way would be greater for those who are paying a relatively high rate of tax than those in lower income groups whose tax rate is lower.

10

Other Factors Affecting Return on Investment

Before proceeding from consideration of the first of the three Rs to turn to the second element, the question of risk, we look in this chapter at some other factors which affect return on investment.

The Effect of Changing Interest Rates

In the last few years, interest rates in the United States and indeed in most countries throughout the world have fluctuated to a far greater extent than in earlier years. In the early 80s many interest rates were at levels as much as three times as high as what was considered normal 5 to 10 years earlier. Some evidence seems to suggest that there has been a semipermanent increase in interest rates. Even after declining from the high levels of the early 80s, interest rates in the second half of 1983 and early 1984 were still about twice as high as the average level of 10 years ago.

So investors now have to take into account not only the question of fluctuating interest rates, but also the fact that interest rates are probably likely to stay more or less on a higher plateau than in the first two or three postwar decades. As those decades were the periods in which so much of the present conventional wisdom in relation to investment decisions was formulated, this means that investors have to look very critically at many old long-accepted investment practices.

On fixed interest investments, changing interest rates have the effect which has been described before: A rise in interest rates results in a decline in the value of similar securities issued earlier at lower interest rates, and vice versa. Expectations about changes in interest rates may be reflected in bond markets.

For equity investments, changing interest rates have a significant effect. First, for the investor who is borrowing to finance part of the cost of his equity investments, the cost of borrowing changes as interest rates change. There is also the other, often overlooked point that, at least in theory, changing interest rates should have an effect on the market value of equity investments. If higher interest rates mean that higher returns are available on fixed interest investments, then, in theory, equity market value should decline to provide a corresponding increase in return on those investments. It doesn't always work this way because of factors such as expectations, market cycles, heavy selling of equity investments, and a whole host of other factors which are discussed at various stages in the book. However, it is a factor which the prudent investor should not ignore.

The large rise in interest rates in the last 5 to 10 years had serious effects on savings and loan organizations and other lenders, who had to pay the high rates to attract new funds to refinance maturing debt while their income on fixed mortgages made some years earlier was at a much lower rate. This had led to some lenders adopting variable mortgages in which interest rates are adjusted from time to time in line with current trends—a practice which is common in many other countries.

Costs of Selecting, Managing, and Reviewing Investments

In general, investments do not manage themselves, and the investor has to allow for that fact in considering the returns from various investments. There are costs involved either in the time of the investor him/herself and/or fees payable to investment advisers, mutual funds, or other professional fund managers. Considerable attention is needed in selecting, managing, and reviewing all investments, but particularly equity investments. In that area, questions as to the trends in the national economy, market cycles, changing investment fashions, the inflow and outflow of funds from foreign investors, and the impact of currency changes on investment markets are a few of the many factors that have to be taken into account.

In fixed interest investments such as bonds, the number of factors to be considered is not as great. But this does not mean that bonds can be bought without any thought about selection or reviewing the portfolio from time to time. Care in selecting investments with a high degree of safety can mean the difference between success and failure. It is also necessary in relation to bond investment to make some estimate as to trends in interest rates in deciding whether to go long or short, that is, whether to invest for a long period to maturity or for a shorter period.

There is also the question as to whether to sell bonds which have risen in value because of a subsequent reduction in interest rates on new securities, or to hold them in the hope of further capital gain.

Today some individual investors find relatively inexpensive microcomputers such as the Apple or the IBM helpful in controlling their investments. There is a good deal of software available to help in this regard, including programs such as Portfolio Evaluation and Reporting System (PEAR). This system keeps portfolio records up to date, provides lists of unrealized and realized capital gain or loss, dissected into short term and long term for tax purposes, adjusts for stock-splits, etc. There are other systems which provide "stock-swapping" facilities to facilitate changes in portfolios, ensuring that stocks which are not meeting the criteria on which their purchase was based are replaced by other stocks.

Some of the computer systems allow for automatic updating of prices through the use of a modem which taps into data banks of services such as the Dow Jones Info Services of Princeton, New Jersey.

Remember the Opportunity Cost Concept

In all aspects of investments—selecting them, reviewing them, and making changes in your portfolio—it is important to remember the opportunity cost concept, which involves recognizing the costs of holding a particular investment, the income and/or capital gain prospects foregone by not investing elsewhere.

It is well to remember that a decision to invest in equities is automatically a decision not to invest in fixed interest investments or direct business investments. The decision to invest in a particular stock is automatically a decision not to invest in other stocks or other types of investments, and to forego the benefits that may be available from those investments.

What is not so widely appreciated is that a decision to continue holding a particular investment is a decision to forego the opportunity of selling that investment at the particular market value reigning at that time. One famous and successful investor is reported to have said that the biggest single reason for his investment success was that he always sold "too soon." He explained that he sold when consideration of opportunity costs justified that decision, even though it may have meant that in the short term a higher profit might have been available later. In the medium and longer term he did much better than those who hesitated to sell for fear that they might miss out on larger profits.

Effect of Currency Changes on Foreign Investments

Today it is very easy for both institutions and individuals to invest in foreign markets. When you invest in foreign markets you have an additional factor which can affect, sometimes quite significantly, your investment return. It is the change in the value of the foreign currency relative to the U.S. currency during the period of your investment.

If the value of the foreign currency increases relative to the U.S. currency during that period, then this is a gain for you. On the other hand, if it declines relative to the U.S. currency, then it is an investment loss.

Those gains or losses could either augment or offset the investment results. So in foreign investments you really have the three components of return, income, and capital gain plus the currency factor.

As currency movements tend to be volatile and at times somewhat unpredictable, this is an important factor which must be given careful thought. Some large investors are able to obtain some sort of a hedge against currency fluctuations if they have the liabilities as well as investment assets in foregin currency. In that event, a movement in the currency in a direction beneficial to foreign investments works the other way in relation to their foreign liabilities. Another way of minimizing the problem of foreign investments is to invest in a mutual fund which places its capital in another country on the basis that a larger mutual fund may be better able to hedge against currency fluctuations and possibly, with better investment and currency evaluation expertise, cope with this problem better than an individual (though you would have to be careful to check that you invest in a fund with a good track record).

Some Nonfinancial Factors

As well as financial factors of investment return, there are some important nonfinancial factors. One is the question of worry. A person who is inclined to worry more than normal about adverse developments should think seriously about having a great portion of his or her money in equity investments that are subject to fluctuation. Although those investments may be preferable on a logical basis, it may be desirable on psychological grounds for that person to have at least a significant part of his or her funds in other investments. There is not much point to facing the prospect of considerable worry which may affect a person's well-being and even his or her or state of health, as that may be too large a cost to pay for what in the long term could be good investment results.

In relation to investment in your own home, the pride of ownership and the security of tenure, the gratification from improving the garden and surrounding of your own home may justify a decision to purchase a home even if economic factors such as high borrowing costs (after allowing for the tax benefit) may tend to point in the other direction.

Some people may like to invest in certain investments for policy reasons not entirely related to cold, hard financial analysis. For example, they may wish to support a local enterprise, or they may wish to support an enterprise which is engaged in pursuing objectives which they thing are important from a social, political, or religious point of view. In considering such questions it is well to remember the difference between a primary and a secondary market. Though we tend to say we are investing in IBM or General Motors or whatever when we buy common stocks, we are really investing in a secondary market. The money we pay for purchase of the stock goes to the seller of that stock. Indirectly it has an effect on the company in whose stock we invest in that if nobody bought the stock its value would decline substantially, and its cost of capital and hence its profits would be affected. But there is not the same effect as when an investment is made directly in providing loan funds to an organization or providing equity capital for a direct business investment.

A Summary of Part Two

In considering return, the first of the three Rs of investing, it is important to recognize the two elements, that is, income and capital gain or loss, and to consider whether the return is stable, variable, or volatile. It is wise to distinguish between actual money and maybe money.

A necessary first step is to understand the time value of money, the use of present value figures, and how to calculate the value of a bond where the current market rate of interest differs from the coupon rate at which the bond was issued. The amount to pay off mortgage debts, compound rates of growth, the significance of compounding, and the reasons why high rates of growth cannot be maintained indefinitely are other aspects of the question. A rule of thumb for compounding calculations, and the formula used, are covered in Chapter 5.

Investors need to have a clear idea of the difference between fixed income and variable income and of the arguments for and against payment of no dividend. Market price at time of purchase can have a crucial effect on income return on equities. Chapter 6 refers also to the range of income on various investments, the means of measuring investment income, the use of income based on market values, and the significance of income for various investors, including those who are primarily interested in capital gain.

Capital gain (or loss), the other component of investment returns, has many faces. There can be good capital gain on "ordinary" investments and less capital gain, or even capital loss, on "good investments." Basically, capital gain or loss comes from two sources: changes in capital value reflecting changes in the earnings of the investment, or changes due to the market applying a different capitalization rate to earnings. Changes can be due to changes in the perception of information as well as to objective changes. Capital values can be affected by changes due to basic economics or changes more directly associated with investment markets, such as market cycles, popularity and disenchantment, fallacies and effective selling, fashions and "the flavor of the month." There can be a different impact on fixed interest and equity investments.

A sensible approach to the question of the impact of taxation on investments decision involves recognizing its significance and thinking in terms of after-tax returns. There is a need to recognize the varying risks in attempts to achieve tax benefits and for a careful check on the honesty, financial soundness, and reliability of managers of tax shelter schemes.

Changing interest rates have a direct effect on the value of fixed interest investments and an indirect effect on equity investments to the extent that changes in yields to compensate for changing interest rates are not offset by other factors. Currency changes can affect foreign investments. There are also nonfinancial factors such as worry about fluctuations in market values and a possible effect on the health of the investor, and pride of ownership and security of tenure in investment in a home. The cost of selecting, reviewing, and managing investments is also relevant. It is important to remember the opportunity cost concept, which is discussed in later chapters.

part 3

The Second R— Risk in Investing

11

More Obvious and Less Obvious Sources of Investment Risk

Why would conservative trustees of a pension fund invest in high risk stocks? That question has been asked many times in the last 10 years, especially by members of pension funds, investors in mutual funds, or others who sold their investments at a time of low stock market values and who were disappointed to find that the amount they received was a good deal less than expected.

The short answer to the question is that the reason for their making those investments is that they did not realize at the time of making the investments that they were high risk investments. Indeed, many of the trustees may have prided themselves on the fact that they did not invest in speculative stocks and concentrated on quality stocks. Perhaps they may have listed the names of well-known, financially strong, highly regarded companies in which they had invested as examples of that "conservative" policy. What they overlooked was that however prestigious a company may be, however competent its management, however highly regarded it may be, investing in the stock of that company can be a speculative investment.

There used to be an old investment saying that an investor is a disappointed speculator—that a person who bought for quick gain and found that the market did not cooperate with his hopes continued to hold the investment for a fairly long period. Perhaps he rationalized his position by saying that he was a person who invested for the medium and long term and was not a trader or speculator. Today, many people who think they are investors are really speculators. Whether they like it or not, the stocks in which they invest, including so-called blue chip stocks, are speculative investments because of the number of investors, including institutions, speculating about future market trends and trying to outguess each other in the market.

How Risk Can Affect Income and Capital

Some risks affect both income and capital. For example, the risk associated with changing business conditions can cause a decline in the earnings of a company (or the net return from a property investment). This can also be reflected in the capital value (remember the point made earlier that, if all other things were equal, capital values would reflect changes in earning rate).

Other risks affect primarily capital value. There have been many cases where earnings have continued to grow, but capital values have declined, probably due to causes associated with investment markets—for example, the swings in the market cycle, or reaction to previous excessive price rises.

Various Categories of Risk

Some people would say that the investment area is a good example of the application of Murphy's Law—if anything can go wrong it will, and generally at the worst possible time. So, when thinking of investment risk a large number of different factors could be involved. However, the major types of risks are generally grouped under the following headings:

1. Business risk—the risk that the business may not do well due to internal factors such as inefficiency, poor management, failure to recognize changing conditions, or external factors such as problems with the whole industry, the economy, or world trade.
2. Financial risk—the risk that a company could get into financial difficulties and perhaps fail because of an unsound financial structure, for example, too much reliance on borrowed funds leading to heavy fixed commitments for interest charges, and repayment of borrowed funds leading to intolerable strains in times of weak business conditions.
3. Market risk—risk associated with market factors such as market cycles, changes in market fashions, or reaction to previous excessive rises or declines.
4. Information or accounting risk—the risk that an investment may not do as well as expected because of a difference between the true situation and that revealed by financial statements of listed companies or figures supplied by vendors of real estate or direct business investments.

Recognition of Various Types of Risk

The above list of investment risks is just about in descending order of the degree of recognition. Business risk is recognized by most investors more or less intuitively. Financial risk is recognized by investment analysts, business executives, and experienced investors who have noticed how highly leveraged companies failed or got into serious trouble in difficult times.

Market risk is not widely recognized. Even experienced investors and many investment advisers tend to overlook it. If market risk were widely recognized, the term *blue chip stocks* would disappear from use. The use of that term is a sign of failure to recognize market risk, because so many of those so-called blue chip stocks, quality stocks, or growth stocks have been disappointing for many investors.

Information or accounting risk is also seldom recognized, even by experienced investors, analysts, and advisers. There is still a lot of truth in the cynical statement that financial statements for many companies are something like bikini swimsuits in that what they reveal is interesting, but what they conceal is vital.

How the Mighty Have Fallen—Some Examples of Market Declines

The point that well-known and highly regarded stocks are not immune to the law of gravity can be seen from the following list showing percentage declines in some well-known stocks in the years between 1969 and 1974.

Stock	Period of Decline	Percentage of Decline
General Motors	1971–1974	62%
Firestone Tire	1969–1974	41
McDonald's Corp.	1972–1974	61
Avon Products	1972–1974	84
IBM	1972–1974	54
Nabisco Brands, Inc.	1972–1974	63
Coca-Cola	1972–1974	65
Sears Roebuck & Co.	1972–1974	63

It would be fair to say that the vast bulk of the significant decline in all those stocks was due to market factor, generally reaction to excessive enthusiasm of an earlier period. It was not due to any collapse in earnings, as many of the stocks maintained their earnings fairly well over the period and others experienced relatively small declines in earnings compared to the declines in stock values.

Accounting Risk

One of the major reasons for accounting risk (the risk that an investment may not be as good as expected because of the difference between the real situation and that revealed by financial statements) is the lack of objectivity in some financial statements and the wide range of alternative accounting treatments that can be used. Though auditors, accountants, and finance people speak of acceptable accounting principles or standards, there are often many alternative accounting treatments for particular items. This means that some directors are inclined to choose those accounting treatments which tend to give a picture of what they would like to have happened during the year rather than what actually happened. There is one fairly simple example of this problem. Some companies, in good years, adopt an extremely conservative attitude to the valuation of inventory, work in progress, or the provision for items such as depreciation of plant and machinery. Then, when they run into a bad year, they adopt a less conservative approach, or perhaps swing toward the other extreme of an overly optimistic approach (possibly arguing that as excessive depreciation had been provided in the accounts of early years, a less than normal provision is needed in the current year). The result of practices such as these is to understate profits in good years and to overstate them in less favorable times. The problem for an investor is that he or she may think the good reported performance in a period of tight business conditions accurately reflects the earning capacity of the company, when it may be due to a substantial degree to the use of the secret reserves created in earlier years.

Some progress has been made toward improved accounting standards, but there is still considerable scope for improvement. So, this is a risk area which investors should keep in mind. It tends to be larger in some companies than others—for example, in companies engaged in construction or civil engineering where some juggling with the figures for work in progress may have a considerable effect on the "bottom line," that is, the earnings available to common stock holders after taxation and after any prior charges such as preference dividends.

Another serious problem in reports of companies is that the accounting profession has not yet completely faced up to the problem of the effect of changing money values. There are currently some moves in this direction but, by and large, financial statements are based on what the accountants call the historic cost concept. For example, fixed assets such as plant and machinery are based on cost price, perhaps some years earlier, after an allowance for depreciation. In times of high inflation such as the early 1980s and part of the 70s, this practice tends to overstate the earning capacity of the business. The reported profits are higher than they would be if depreciation was related not to the cost price of some years earlier, but to a higher replacement cost figure. The problem is increased by the fact that the overstated earnings are then related in terms of a percentage on shareholders' funds or assets used to a figure which understates the situation in terms of the current value of those assets.

Risk of Inadequate Analysis and Advice

In addition to the four basic types of risks referred to above, investors also face the problem of inadequate analysis and advice on investments. This is particularly relevant in stock markets. Nearly all of the comments on stocks tend to ignore realities, including the significant and sometimes dominant effects of market factors such as cyclical movements, changes in market fashions, etc. They also tend to overlook the importance of relative costs (the cost of equities compared with other investments, a matter which is discussed in detail in later chapters). Frequently, comments about investments, including those by investment specialists, do not make sufficient allowance for the problems of accounting and information costs referred to above. Another common error is to assume that stock market trends accurately forecast trends in the economy. This implies that if the economy is likely to perform well during a particular year, then the purchase of stock at the beginning of that year or just before it is likely to be rewarding. The facts are that whatever improvement may take place in the economy could already have been anticipated and perhaps grossly overanticipated by the market. That is why periods of a buoyant economy and increasing earnings for listed companies are often accompanied by sideways or downward movements in the stock market. (The second half of 1983 is a good recent example.)

Risks Associated with Interest Rate Changes

The sharp movements in interest rates in the last few years have made investors more conscious of the effect of interest rate changes on investments—the direct effect on fixed interest stocks such as bonds, and the indirect effect on stocks to the extent to which changes in interest rates are reflected by changes in price earnings multiples or dividend yields of listed stocks.

Prudent investors need to take this factor into account in order to make an assessment of it or to seek advice on this particular point in making their investment decisions.

12

The Paradox of High Risk
in "Good Investments"

"It seems to me that all they want to do is to go broke gracefully." That was a comment made by a business executive expressing his frustration at the failure of a farming group to adopt new improved management and marketing techniques which would have involved a significant change in their way of life. In the investment world, a somewhat similar comment could be made that the traditional investment wisdom seems to work on the assumption that it does not matter if you lose money through investing in the stock of well-known companies, the so-called blue chips, the growth stocks, or other "darlings of the market."

The Basic Realities of Investment Markets

Some investment analysts become so immersed in the detailed analysis of company earnings, estimating projected earnings for the future, and studying the management standards of companies that they subconsciously seem to think that making an investment is like giving a seal of approval to the stock. But the harsh realities are that when you invest in equities, you are committing your funds into a market which can be affected by a wide range of factors including greed and avarice, enthusiasm at some times, panic at others.

This is particularly so in the stock market, which tends to be more volatile because it is more widely publicized and more liquid. If the price of a stock declines after you have purchased it, you lose money whether the name of that stock is International Business Machines or Boondocks Bargain Bazaar. The point has already been made in an earlier chapter that it is possible to lose money on what are called good stocks and to make money on less prestigious stocks.

So much depends on timing. The list of declines in the previous chapter shows that over a few years significant declines, many well over 50 percent, occurred in the price of very well-known stocks.

Growing Speculation in So-Called Quality Investments

"Wall Street people," said a businessman recently, "are like a herd of cattle. They always seem to be stampeding into the market or out of it." That is a reasonably fair comment, because the emphasis on reporting stock market movements and an analysis of short-term performance of various institutions has tended to produce that effect. Because markets are highly priced relative to other investments, investment institutions' and advisers' better judgment may tell them to stay out of the market for a while when a buying rush commences. But after it has gone on for a little while they fear that they will be left behind, and so they climb on the bandwagon.

The result is that when a more sober analysis would have suggested caution, perhaps taking a profit by reducing holdings in the market at that time, so-called informed opinion tends simply to jump on the bandwagon, thus accelerating the swings in the market. To put it another way, there is far too much evidence today of the selling tail wagging the sound investment dog. Unfortunately, that speculation now tends to affect all sections of the market. The days when wide swings in market prices were limited to the "penny dreadfuls" low-priced stocks have gone. It is true that those stocks may be somewhat more speculative and more volatile than the stock of well-established companies. One way or another all stocks, including the most prestigious, are now subject to significant speculative influence.

The Madness of Crowds

In 1932, financier and successful investor Bernard Baruch wrote a foreword to a new edition of a book, the study of which he said had saved him millions. Was it a book on investing? No. Then was it a book on accounting or finance or economics? No, the book which Bernard Baruch said had saved him millions was not on any of those subjects.

The book to which he referred was *Extraordinary Popular Delusions and the Madness of Crowds* by Charles Mackay. (A recent edition was published in 1980 by Harmony Books, New York.) In writing the foreword for the October 1932 edition Baruch quoted Schiller, who said, "Anyone taken as an individual is tolerably sensible and reasonable—as a member of a crowd he at once becomes a blockhead." Andrew Tobias, the writer of the foreword to the 1980 edition, goes on to say, "There are lynch mobs and there are crusades; there are runs on banks and there are fires where, if only people had not panicked they would have all escaped with their lives. There was the hussle, not so long ago, where large groups of young people learned to dance in lemming-like unision . . . and there was the mass suicide in Jonestown."

The comments of Andrew Tobias and Bernard Baruch should be remembered by every investor. The study of that book, particularly the first 100 pages or so dealing with the South Sea Bubble and the tulip mania in Holland in the 17th century, has important lessons for the investor about what some people call mob psychology.

When there is a boom in the stock market, in real estate, in gold, or whatever, sales people, financial institutions, and analysts, in the enthusiasm of the moment, say that this boom will continue and that it differs from other booms of the past. The plain facts of the matter are that with every boom since the South Sea Bubble, whether it was the Florida land boom of the 1920s, the stock market boom of the late 20s, the boom in conglomerates and so-called "go go" mutual funds (which sadly went went), or the boom in gambling stocks in the 70s, investors need to remember two points. One is that the law of gravity has not been repealed and what goes up generally comes down, often when least expected by the market generally. The second is the hangover analogy— just as a late party tonight may mean a worse hangover tomorrow, so a long or extreme boom can be followed by a more severe slump.

The Bigger Fool Theory, but Don't Be Later than Next-to-Last

There is a reference elsewhere in the text to what is called the bigger fool theory. This theory says that when there is a boom you can make a profit by buying at a foolish price because before too long a bigger fool will come along and offer you an even more foolish price. But the problem is that the supply of fools is not unlimited. So the smart thing is to ensure that you are no later than the next-to-last fool when the crunch comes and the market goes into a severe slump.

13

How Each Investor Should Decide on the Right Risk Category

A cynic has said that averages can be misleading because a person with one foot in the fire and the other in a bucket of ice is, on the average, at a comfortable temperature, but that may not help him very much. It is little consolation for an investor who purchases real estate or common stock at a time which happens to be the peak of a cycle and sells it some time later at a low point in the cycle at a considerable loss to be told that in the medium to long term most investors in real estate and common stocks have done well. Because many people who sell investments and many others who have fallen in love with a particular type of investment seldom talk of the risk involved, it is important for investors to consider this question carefully. In doing so, they need to consider it from their particular viewpoint.

Why This Fundamental Question Is Often Overlooked

Apart from the less than objective outlook of those who are selling particular types of investments or those who become extremely enthusiastic about particular investments, there are other reasons for the question of risk not receiving anywhere near the attention it warrants. One is the tendency for the investment world to think that a constant rise is the natural state of affairs for popular investments such as real estate or common stocks. This leads to the thought that any decline in market values is a temporary mental aberration and that the market will soon come to its senses. Apple pie, motherhood, and a rising Dow Jones Index have come to be regarded as matters on which there should be no debate.

Another reason is that the realities of short- and medium-term market movements may be overshadowed by longer term movements or the popular perception of longer term movements.

Over a period of many years, there may have been a net gain in the value of a particular investment from, say, $1,000 to $1,800. So the first impression is that there has been a significant rise, which is true in terms of the net movement. But examination may show that the net movement is comprised of two elements—an increase from $1,000 to $2,500, followed by a decline from $2,500 to $1,800. At some times and in some investments, the more recent experience, the decline from $2,500 to $1,800, may be closer to what could be expected in the medium-term future than the earlier large rise or even the longer term rise from $1,000 to $1,800.

Two Basic Questions

In considering the question of risk, there are two basic questions which investors should consider. They are:

1. What general degree of risk exposure is appropriate, that is, should the general approach be one of low risk, medium risk, high risk, or very high risk?
2. What is the maximum risk exposure to which funds should be exposed?

The latter point is particularly important. When we insure our homes against the risk of fire, we know that statistically the probability of our home being destroyed by fire is relatively low, but we do not on that account decide not to insure it or to insure it for only a portion of its value. We want to be covered against the worst possible event, the complete destruction of the building. So we would need full insurance coverage including replacement costs, which may be higher than the cost of the building when we purchased it, and associated costs including temporary accommodation while awaiting rebuilding.

In investment, something like the same approach is needed. Even if we know that on the basis of past experience there is an 85 percent probability of an investment producing gain and only a 15 percent probability that it will result in a loss, we have to consider the possibility of loss. We need to recognize that risk and take measures such as a spread of investment, careful selection, and other matters discussed in later chapters to minimize our risk. We also need to consider the maximum degree of risk which we can accept in our particular situation. For some investors such as those with limited capital to invest and limited income from other sources, this may mean that risk exposure has to be set at a low figure which would prevent those investors from investing even a portion of their funds in medium risk or higher risk investments.

Particular Factors to Be Considered

In considering the question of risk, the following factors are important:

1. *Age group.* Generally speaking, younger and middle-aged people can accept a higher degree of risk because they would have the opportunity of building up their capital again after any adverse investment experience. This opportunity may not be available to older people, whose income earning period has ended or is close to an end.

2. *Other income.* A person with adequate income from a salary, a business or profession, or other sources can afford to be more venturesome than a person with little or no income from other sources who is dependent on the investments for all or the bulk of his or her normal income.

3. *Overall finances.* The total assets and liabilities and net assets are relevant because a person with a large net worth can generally afford to take a higher risk with at least some of his or her capital than a person with limited capital who cannot really afford to lose any of it.

4. *Cash needs.* Future needs for such purposes as education, purchase of a home or business, prolonged trips to other countries, or any other factor creating a need for cash is important. The person who knows that he or she has a significant cash need that would involve the sale of investments during the next few years would generally require a greater proportion of low risk investments and a smaller proportion in the medium risk investments subject to market fluctuation than would otherwise be appropriate (because cash needs may prevent him or her from riding out any downswing and waiting for the market cycle to move up again).

5. *Psychology.* A person investing in medium or high risk investments, remembering that some of the so-called blue chips are high risk investments, need to have the right mental attitude. Such people need to realize that they will go through periods when markets move against them and that however skilled they are some of their decisions will not be correct. Those who cannot face up to that problem or who are likely to worry unduly about adverse market movements may need to adopt a lower risk policy on psychological grounds than would otherwise be appropriate.

Risk of Other Income

If the other income earned by an investor is fairly stable, for example, in a secure position or a well-established profession, he or she could afford to take more risks than a person who does not have a permanent position or is in a business subject to significant fluctuations, such as farming, where changing markets and weather conditions can have serious effects.

Present Investments

A person whose present investment portfolio has a lower risk than it would be reasonable for him or her to accept could more readily consider a medium or high risk investment than a person in approximately the same overall situation who already has a larger part of his or her funds invested in medium and high risk investments than is appropriate to the situation.

The Portfolio Effect

The latter point is extremely important. All investment decisions need to be made within the context of the overall portfolio. Hence, an investor considering the purchase of a medium to high risk investment, who already has a more than reasonable proportion in that area, should refrain from making that purchase—unless he or she also sells some of the existing investments in that category to reduce the overall risk of the portfolio.

Individual Investors and Risk Category

We now turn to consider the various risk categories which are relevant and appropriate for particular investors. The groupings discussed below are primarily by way of illustration of the basic principles involved. They are not completely precise. Moreover, it is necessary to consider all of the factors outlined above. For example, as a general principle older investors would tend to adopt a lower risk posture than younger investors. But an older investor who has large amounts of capital and adequate income from other sources could afford to take a higher risk than a younger person with limited capital and little or no income from other sources, or income which is uncertain and variable.

Subject to those reservations, the risk categories for various investors are discussed below.

Low Risk Investors

In general, the investors who should adopt low risk policies with all or most of the funds in low risk investments would include the following:

1. Older investors with little or no working life ahead of them to rebuild capital after any reverse.
2. Investors with limited capital for investment and relatively low net worth; investors whose income from other sources is low or uncertain; investors whose personality, state of health, or other factors would mean that the worry of equity investments, including adverse

market fluctuations, might create serious mental and possibly physical health problems for them.

3. Investors who know that they will need all or a major part of their invested capital for planned cash needs, such as the purchase of a home, education, or other items within the next two or three years or so.

High to Very High Risk Investors

At the other end of the scale, the investors who could afford to adopt high to very high risk policies would include the following:

1. Young to middle-aged people with many years of working life ahead of them who have the opportunity of rebuilding their capital out of savings after any adverse investment experience.
2. Investors with large amounts available for investment and large net worth.
3. Investors with more than adequate income for normal needs available from other sources which are fairly reliable and assured.
4. Investors with negligible cash needs in the next two or three years for any special projects.
5. Those with the psychology, experience, and skill to understand the risk associated with high and very high risk investments, including futures trading, who can take market reverses in their stride without undue worry.

Investors in that group described above could consider having a fairly significant amount of their funds in high to very high risk investments because the loss of a significant part of their total invested capital would not spell financial ruin for them. They may wish to limit their investment in low risk investments to a small portion as a sort of safe haven in difficult market times—with the intention of also using those investments as a temporary refuge for funds that otherwise would be invested in medium and high risk investments at times when those markets appear high and vulnerable to possible decline.

Medium Risk Investors

Medium risk investors would be those who fit in between the two extremes outlined above. These people could afford to consider placing some of their funds in medium to high risk investments, but they would have to maintain a significant part in lower risk investment areas in the interests of a balanced portfolio appropriate to their particular needs.

Obviously, there is a large range in this medium area. At the lower end of the range, there would be investors who are just a little better able to afford investment risks than those in the low risk category described above. At the other end of the scale, there would be investors in the medium risk area who would be able to face investment risks almost as great as those which would be appropriate for investors in the high to very high risk investment area.

Different Degrees of Risk for Various Parts of the Portfolio

Because it is the overall portfolio that is important, the risk must be seen in relation to that portfolio. This means that, for example, medium risk investors may not necessarily seek to place all of their funds in medium risk investments. They could place some in low risk investments as a "sheet anchor" for the portfolio, some in medium risk investments, and some in high risk investments. The portion in high risk investments would need to be limited to a small portion of the overall total. Basically, the concept we are discussing here is a type of weighted average risk for the whole portfolio—an average of the risk of the various investments weighted according to the proportion of the total portfolio in the different categories.

An Attempt to Measure Risk

Some years ago I developed the concept of relative risk rating as a means of trying to be a little more objective in relation to the risk of various investments. On the basis of considering the worst possible situation (as the home owner does in insuring his or her home against complete destruction by fire), the relative risk rating is a measure of the worst situation, based on past experience over the period of the last 20 years. In other words, it measures the risk by looking at the loss if you purchased an investment at the high point and sold at the low point during that period.

It does not necessarily follow that past experience is a reliable indicator of the future. But until some more reliable measure is available, this measure, though far from perfect, is a step in the right direction.

So that the measure is on a practical and fairly easily understood basis, the relative risk rating looks at the amount of capital remaining after an investment suffered the worst possible experience (buying at the very top and selling at the very bottom). It is arrived at by dividing the capital invested by the amount of capital remaining after sale in the worst possible situation. For example, if the total decline was 50 percent, there would be $50 remaining for each $100 invested. Dividing $50 into $100 gives a risk factor of 2. If there was no loss at all in the worst possible situation, for example, short-term investments with a high safety ranking, then the capital remaining of $100 divided into the capital invested of $100 gives a rating of 1.

At the other extreme, volatile investments such as some of the "penny dreadfuls" or volatile mineral exploration stocks which declined by 90 percent would have a relative risk rating of 10 (original capital of $100 divided by capital remaining of $10). (If you refer back to the list of well-known stocks in Chapter 11 where declines range from 41 to 84 percent, the range of relative risk rating for those stocks would be from 1.69 to 6.25.)

The Relative Risk Rating of the Stock Market

The relative risk rating figure outlined above can be calculated for major markets, such as the stock market. If the Dow Jones Industrial Index were used in this exercise, the relative risk rating on the basis of the experience in the last 20 years would be calculated as follows:

$$
\begin{array}{lrr}
\text{Peak} & 1973 = & 1{,}052 \\
\text{Low point} & 1974 = & 578 \\
\text{Relative risk rating } (1{,}052 \div 578) = & 1.82
\end{array}
$$

Relative Risk Rating of a Portfolio

The relative risk rating of a portfolio can be calculated by arriving at the weighted average relative risk rating as set out below:

Investments	Amount	Percentage of Total	Real Risk Rating	Weighting
Short-term bonds	$ 4,000	8%	1.0	0.08
Medium-term bonds	4,000	8	1.1	0.09
Long-term bonds	12,000	24	1.5	0.36
Common stocks	15,000	30	1.8	0.54
Gold	15,000	30	2.9	0.87
Total	$50,000	100%		1.94

Those calculations show that the portfolio having that composition would have a relative risk rating of 1.94. The third column shows the amount of the various investments as a percentage of the total. The fourth column shows the relative risk rating of the various investments, and the weighting in the last column is arrived at by applying that percentage to the relative risk rating for that category of investment.

The above figures would show that a portfolio constituted in that way has a relative risk rating of 1.94. That would just about place it in the medium risk category with the high risk investment in gold, with a relative risk rating of 2.9, being offset by 40 percent of the total portfolio being in the low and low to medium category: short-term bonds, medium-term bonds, and long-term bonds with risk ratings of 1.0, 1.1, and 1.5 respectively.

Analysis of the portfolio in this way from time to time is useful, as it shows whether the weighted relative risk rating for the whole portfolio is in line with what is appropriate from a policy point of view. If the portfolio above belonged to a person who should adopt a low risk investment policy, it would call for some changes to reduce the investments in the high risk category and to increase those in the low risk category.

Different Risk Exposure at Various Stages of Market Cycles

The relative risk rating and the comments on risk above are an attempt to classify various types of investment in risk categories. Because of market cycles, equity investments would tend to have a higher degree of risk when markets have risen sharply, relative costs are high, and there could be a reaction from recent rises. On the other hand, the relative risk rating would be lower if the market had experienced a significant decline and had shown some signs of stabilizing and then starting to recover. Because of these facts of investment life, investors should not ignore market realities. In considering whether the relative risk rating of their portfolio is appropriate, they have to consider not only whether the risk rating from the viewpoint of static analysis regardless of market cyclical position is appropriate, but whether the present position of the market in its cyclical movement significantly affects the risk.

14

Various Investments Classified According to Risk

In Chapter 13 we looked at the question of risk from the viewpoint of the investor and the various types of investors for whom low risk, medium risk, high risk, or very high risk would be appropriate. In this chapter we turn to look at the question of risk from the viewpoint of investments and the classifying of investments according to their risk category.

Classifying Risk after Normal Safeguards

The comments in this chapter on the risk of various investments are made on the assumption that investors would take normal precautions to minimize risk. These would include a spread of investments so that too many eggs are not in the one basket, careful selection of investments to minimize risk, and various other matters which are discussed in later chapters. That selection process, if properly carried out by the investor or an adviser, would limit the risk to which the investor is exposed through companies likely to face adverse business conditions, the effects of bad management, or possible problems including failure through an unsound financial structure. For the remainder of the comments in this chapter, we assume that these and other precautions discussed in later chapters have been taken.

A General Principle

Though there are some exceptions, it is fairly true to say that as a general principle, investments which produce a reasonable income return in relation to interest rates and returns available on other investments, tend to have a relatively low risk. On the other hand, with investments which produce little income or negative income (for example, vacant land where there is no income but an outgoing on payments for property taxes and other holding charges) the risk is relatively great.

In the area of property investments, income-producing property is not nearly as volatile as vacant land. The income-producing property would generally not rise as spectacularly in booms and would not fall as dramatically in declines as would the value of vacant land or other property being held for development producing little or no income. This is a significant point. If all investors were to realize that the larger the gap between the income returned from an investment and current interest rates, then generally, the larger the investment risk, there would not be such spectacular losses when market reactions set in after equity investments have been pushed to completely unrealistic prices in relation to their earning capacity and current interest rates. If investment advisers and investment institutions became more wary of those investments where the yield gap was becoming so great, the performance of many investments including some so-called blue chips stock would be a lot less volatile and a lot less worrysome for investors.

Very Low Risk Investments

In this category, there would be the following investments:

1. Deposits with banks or savings and loan companies which are covered by Federal Deposit Insurance Corporation protection.
2. Investments in federal government securities or the securities of government-guaranteed bodies, such as G.N.M.A. and F.N.M.A.
3. Short-term loans to selected companies which offer a high safety ranking because of the margin provided by shareholders' funds or other providers of funds which rank behind the loan with a good earnings record and cash flow.
4. Short-term mortgage loans to individuals or corporations in a sound financial position.

Low Risk Investments

In the low risk category, there are the following investments:

1. Medium-term bonds of companies with good earning capacity, a sound financial structure in terms of the backing of shareholders' funds, and well-balanced spread of maturities on liabilities.
2. Medium-term mortgages to individuals or corporations in a sound financial position.
3. Convertible notes, if purchased at a price where the interest return

would maintain a reasonably good market value even if the value of the stock of the relevant company were to decline because of changed earnings conditions, market cycles, or other factors.

Low to Medium Risk Area

In this intermediate area between low risk and medium risk would be fixed interest investments such as corporate or government bonds, or mortgage loans for a long term in the 5- to 20-year range. Even though the loans may be safe from the viewpoint of payment of interest and repayment of capital, because of government guarantee or the sound financial position of corporate or individual borrowers, these investments have to be placed in the low to medium risk category because of risks associated with interest rate changes. Now that we have reached a stage of semipermanent, relatively high interest rates compared with 10 to 20 years ago, this risk may not be so great. The reason is that the adverse effect of a change in interest rates on the capital value of securities issued earlier is more significant when interest rates are low.

For example, if interest rates were to rise from 4 percent to 6 percent, fixed interest investments for a long period of 20 years or more issued earlier at 4 percent would suffer a decline in capital value of nearly 30 percent (because 2 percent is one third of the new rate of 6 percent), but a change of 2 percent, from 12 percent to 14 percent, on securities with a period to maturity of 20 years or more would produce a loss around 10 percent, because 2 percent is only one seventh of the new rate of 14 percent.

The important point to note here is that this interest rate risk applies to all fixed interest investments regardless of the safety ranking of the borrower.

The change in capital value of previously issued securities due to changes in interest rates available on new securities is dependent on two factors. These are, first, the significance of the change in interest rates (discussed above), and second, the period to maturity. As pointed out in an earlier chapter, the change in capital value for any given change in interest rates is greater for investments with 10, 15, or 20 years to maturity than for investments with 1 or 2 years to maturity. So this risk can be minimized considerably by limiting investments to the medium term of a few years.

Medium Risk Investments

In the medium risk investment area are those investments where market forces play a significant part. This includes the whole equity area including shares, property, and commodities. More specifically, the medium risk category would include the following types of investments:

1. Income-producing property.
2. Common stocks (except for some very low-yielding stocks that tend to have more volatile market movements, which would put them in a high risk category).
3. Long-term fixed interest investments in the event of a significant change in interest rates.

High Risk Investments

Remembering the point made earlier that, in general, investments which produce a relatively low income return tend to involve higher risk, the investments in this category would include the following:

1. Vacant land or income-producing property purchased for redevelopment producing fairly low income until redevelopment has been completed.
2. High priced stocks producing low income which tend to have greater downside risk because of more volatile market movements in the absence of the stabilizing factor of a reasonable income.
3. Commodities such as gold, silver, and other items that have volatile price movements, partly due to speculation and partly due to changes in supply and demand and expectations on those items (here we are referring to direct purchase of commodities—futures trading in commodities which involves a higher risk is in the next category of investments).
4. Any equity investment purchased at a time when markets have experienced a very high rise with the possibility or the probability of a significant decline being imminent.

Very High Risk Investments

In the very high risk investments would be the following:

1. Common stock with greater than normal fluctuations, including mining stocks (partly due to fluctuations in commodity values), mineral exploration stocks, very low priced stocks (the "penny dreadfuls"), or venture capital type investments in new operations that may do very well if fortune smiles on them and very badly if it does not.
2. Futures trading where the leverage effect of speculating on margins (originally investing as a deposit an amount which is perhaps only 5

or 10 percent of the value of the underlying contract) multiplies the up and down swings of commodity prices, which themselves are very volatile.

3. The more speculative type of real estate investments, including the purchase of large areas of nonurban land that may produce good gains if it is subsequently rezoned to urban land and successful develoment takes place, but a significant loss if that does not occur.

4. Common stocks with more than normal risks, such as very highly leveraged companies which could fail in the event of a downturn in business conditions, preventing them from meeting their high fixed charges on debts, or industries likely to face extremely adverse conditions from imminent changes in technology, changes in tariffs and other factors affecting imports, or changes in government regulations.

Seeing Risk in Perspective

It is well to remember that the above comments broadly relate to different types of investments to indicate the general risk category for various types of investment. That risk can be increased or decreased according to the care or lack of it given by the investor to such matters as a reasonable spread of investment, constant review of one's investments, obtaining full information from objective sources before making decisions, and other matters discussed elsewhere in the text.

15

How Borrowing
Can Affect
Investment Risk

One of the best reasons for not making any particular investment is not being able to afford it. This simple common sense principle is often ignored by investors who overcommit themselves, generally in wild enthusiasm for a particular type of investment during a boom. This does not mean that investors should completely refrain from borrowing. Borrowing within reasonable limits can improve investment results. So making an investment which involves prudent and sensible borrowing certainly does not conflict with the statement that one should not make an investment which one cannot afford.

Benefits from Borrowing

The benefits that come from sensible borrowing are listed below:

1. *Leverage.* This is the multiplying effect on capital gain. For example, if a property or other investment is purchased with the investor providing half the capital and borrowing the remaining half, an increase in value of 25 percent on that property works out at a gain of 50 percent on the capital invested. If two thirds of the cost were borrowed and one third financed by the investor's capital, the multiplying factor would be 3 so that a 25 percent increase in the value of the property would mean a capital gain on invested funds of 75 percent.
2. *Tax shelters.* In some property and other investments, interest on borrowed funds may reduce that investment income to a small figure or even a negative result to be offset against other taxable income of the investor (with the benefits of the borrowing coming from capital gains subject to a lower tax rate or possibly higher

income in later years after an investor has retired with a lower overall income and hence lower marginal tax rate).
3. *Wider scope.* The additional funds obtained through borrowing may make possible investments that would otherwise not have been practicable.
4. *Earlier investment.* Borrowing may make investment possible sooner than would have been the case if the investor had to wait for availability of funds from sale of other investments, sale of a business, or other sources.
5. *Current opportunities.* Borrowing may make it possible for an investor to take advantage of current opportunities such as a new issue of stock, investments available at lower than normal prices, or participation in an investment opportunity available only for a short period. Without borrowing it may not be possible to participate in those investment opportunities.
6. *Utilizing assets.* Use of borrowed funds may obviate the need to sell assets, which may be undesirable from an investment point of view or from other viewpoints, especially in the case of an investor's home. Borrowing can enable the investor to continue enjoying the use of those assets while still having funds available for other investments or other purposes.

Some astute investors have used the last of the benefits listed above effectively by borrowing against the increasing equity in the value of the home to make profitable investments.

The Risk Involved and Possible Problems

The degree of risk associated with borrowing can be minimized by the measures discussed later in the chapter. Any borrowing involves some additional risk compared to the situation when no borrowed funds are used. It is well to remember that the commitment to pay interest and repay borrowed funds at the stated time is actual money, but the benefits from an investment in which the borrowed funds are applied is in the category of "maybe money." Whether the investment produces the capital gain expected, a low amount of capital gain, or even results in a loss of capital is uncertain, but the commitments in relation to borrowed funds are certain.

In an earlier chapter dealing with different types of risk, we referred to financial risk—the risk that an investment may be disappointing because the company in which stock is purchased fails or gets into trouble through being unable to meet high fixed charges on loans in times of difficult business conditions. For the investor who borrows significant amounts, the obligation to meet fixed interest payments and repayment of capital on the due date could provide serious problems if investment market conditions are adverse.

The major risks and problems involved in borrowing beyond reasonable limits include the following:

1. Serious financial problems for the investor and even the possibility of bankruptcy if conditions are severe.
2. The possibility of forced sales through having to sell investments to meet commitments at times when markets are temporarily depressed, without the option of continuing to hold for recovery that would be available to the investor without high commitments.
3. Possible loss of opportunities to go into other investments because of inadequate available cash due to commitments in relation to loans.
4. Possible worry and concern and a good deal of time spent on "putting out fires," including rearrangements of loans or borrowing temporary funds to meet commitments.

How to Limit the Risks and Problems of Borrowing

Set out below is a list of actions which investors can take to reduce the risk of borrowing and to limit the possible problems that may arise:

1. Limit total liabilities, including possible existing debts such as home mortgages, to a figure which is reasonable in relation to total assets (generally it is wise to limit borrowings to 50 percent of total assets) and which is also reasonable in relation to the income and cash flow of the investor.
2. See that cash flow from other sources such as salary, business or professional income, or other investments is adequate to meet at least part of the interest and repayment commitments on borrowings for investment purposes. This should ensure that no serious problems would arise even if the earnings and cash flow on the investment for which the borrowing was made failed to come up to expectations.
3. Have a balanced maturity pattern with medium- to long-term borrowings to finance long-term investments or equity investments which may have to be held for a long term in the event of prolonged market declines. It is necessary to avoid the temptation to borrow short at relatively low interest rates and invest long.

4. Consider carefully the timing of borrowings, avoiding hurried borrowings at a time of very high interest rates or tight money conditions. There is still some truth in the old saying that the time to borrow funds is when you don't really need them.
5. Maintain adequate cash reserve or access to funds through credit lines with banks or other institutions for any sudden cash needs due to serious damage to a home or business from natural disasters that may not be fully covered by insurance, emergency medical expenses, or other items.
6. Watch investments more closely once you have commenced to borrow because of the greater risk involved.

The above principles may need to be modified to fit in with the particular circumstances, but they constitute a good general approach to the question of prudent borrowing.

16

Means of Controlling, Reviewing, and Reducing Risk

Turning from means of reducing risk and limiting problems on borrowings for investment purposes, we look now at the question of controlling, reviewing, and reducing risks generally in relation to investments.

Clear Positive Recognition

On the principle that the problem least likely to be solved is the one of which we are not aware, the first important step in relation to the matter of investment risk is to recognize it clearly and positively. As well as recognizing the risk that the company whose stock we purchase may get into serious difficulties or fail, or a property or business investment may fall far short of our expectations, it is also necessary to remember the other types of risks which are often overlooked in investment discussions. These include the following:

1. Investment market risk, including the risk of substantial decline in market value of most prestigious stocks or prime property due to factors such as market cycles, changes in investment fashions, and changes in the inflow or outflow of a foreign portfolio invested in a particular market. There is the need to remember the difference between actual money and maybe money.
2. Recognition that description of a stock as blue chip does not mean that it is a safe haven for an investor's funds, as many of these stocks have volatile market movements and involve relatively high risk.
3. Remember the effect of timing on investment risks and that the investments which are most popular at a particular time are often those involving the highest risk, because they could be vulnerable

to sharp decline in a market reaction to previous excessive enthusiasm.

4. Changing sentiment and public reaction to particular industries or the products of industries, including problems faced by utilities, mining companies, and others in relation to action by conservationists on environmental questions.

5. The interest rate risk in relation to fixed interest investments, especially long-term investments, or changes in interest rates in later years may have a significant effect on capital value.

6. Beware of the advice that when you are on a good thing you should stick to it, because a "good thing" in terms of a stock which has performed much better than average may involve higher risks to the investor—both because it may be vulnerable to more significant decline and because its high rise may have increased its percentage of one's overall portfolio to a higher figure so that the decline would be more significant than in previous times.

A Definite Policy on Risk

There are really two essential aspects of this question. The first is for the investor to decide what is the appropriate risk category for him or her; low risk, medium risk, high risk, or very high risk. This involves a consideration of the various matters discussed in Chapter 13.

The second important element is to consider the maximum risk to which the investment portfolio can safely be exposed. Generally the investors in what might be called the low risk category—those who are getting on in years, those with limited capital or limited income from other sources, or those dependent on investments for all or most of their income—may need to limit risk exposure considerably. In the extreme case of the investor with no income from other sources and a limited amount of capital, it may be necessary to set the maximum risk exposure at almost nil. This would mean that he or she would have to concentrate on investments such as low risk short- to medium-term fixed interest investments.

Having made a policy decision on risk, it is important that investors should act on that policy rather than on the mood of the moment in various investment markets. If investment policy considerations warrant a low risk investment policy, then the investors adopting the policy have to face up to the fact that at times when medium and high risk investments are performing well and producing good results they will not participate in those gains. (Their time will probably come when a downturn in the market occurs and those who were previously shouting from the rooftops about their gains become eloquently silent about the severe decline in the capital value of their investments.)

An Adequate but Not Excessive Spread of Investment

The old saying that it is not a good idea to put too many eggs in one basket is relevant in relation to investment risk. Investment should be spread so that if one particular investment faces severe problems, the effect on the overall portfolio is limited. There is a good deal to be said for limiting the amount invested in any relatively low risk fixed interest investment to no more than about 15 percent of one's total portfolio. Investments in medium to high risk investments such as equities should have a lower percentage, perhaps in the 5 to 10 percent range for any one investment.

The idea of a spread of investment is no exception to the statement that it is possible to have too much of a good thing. If the process of seeking spread and diversification is carried too far it can create other problems. One is that portfolios should be fairly well consolidated—with sufficient stocks to provide reasonable spread but limited to a number which can be managed effectively.

For most individual investors, this would generally mean somewhere between 6 and 15 separate investments. If the number of investments for each is 30, 40, or 50 or more, it is far more difficult for the investor to keep track of them, watch them properly, and make sound decisions concerning changes of investments whenever warranted. There are also additional costs involved, because every additional investment means one more entry in your records, one more dividend or interest check to deposit and to record. It may also mean that brokerage costs are higher than they should be because of dealing in smaller individual parcels than would be appropriate.

Increasing spread beyond reasonable limits does not do very much to increase the safety of the portfolio. A portfolio with 30 stocks may not enjoy much greater benefit from spread than a portfolio with 10 to 12 stocks. Moreover, some of the additional stocks may virtually be carbon copies of those already in the portfolio and subject to pretty much the same sort of risk.

Selection of Investments

A person who selects investments carefully or has the selection process done by an investment adviser or by managers of mutual funds will generally face smaller risks than a person who makes haphazard investments without any thought as to the risk involved in the various investments.

Essentially, any investment selection involves looking at the positive aspects of the investment: its earning capacity, its scope for capital gain, and any other features that make it attractive to an investor, such as a nonfinancial benefit of helping to develop business in a certain area or to promote some other objectives. The second question, then, is to look at the risk to which the stock is exposed. Ultimately, the most suitable investment is the one which offers the best combination of return (income and capital gain) in relation to risk. An investment involving relatively high risk that is likely to produce returns about the same as other investments with lower risk would generally be considered not attractive to a prudent investor.

In considering the selection of investments, keeping risks to reasonable limits involves a consideration of the various types of risk. These were described earlier as business risk, financial risk, market risk, accounting or information risk, and the risk of effects on investments due to changes in interest rates.

Sensitivity Analysis

In selecting investments and indeed in reviewing them from time to time, there is scope for use of a technique that is now widely used in business management: sensitivity analysis. This involves seeing how sensitive the planned results of an investment would be to changes in some of the more important variables. In a property investment, these variables would include interest rate paid on borrowed funds, vacancy rate, operational costs, and so on. Sensitivity analysis involves recalculating expected results on the basis of specific changes in key variables. The analysis produces answers to questions such as what would be the effect if rent lost through vacancies and/or concessions to attract tenants were to increase from X to Y, or if costs of the property increase from X to Y, or there was a certain increase in interest rates on borrowed funds.

Even a relatively simple approach making some assumptions as to possible changes in key variables can be helpful. Today, the use of readily available software such as "Visicalc" on microcomputers like the Apple, IBM, and other popular makes facilitates the task of sensitivity analysis a good deal.

An illustration of a simple form of sensitivity analysis is set out in an appendix to this chapter.

Periodical Review

A periodical review is necessary to keep risk within reasonable limits for two reasons. One is that there can be changes in the situation of an investor; for example, he or she may be approaching retirement or a significant change in earnings from other sources, or his/her commitments in terms of dependents may have increased or decreased. The total amount of capital available to the investor may have changed.

The second reason to make periodical reviews desirable is that there can be changes in the situation of the investments. This could include changes from low points to high points in the investment cycle, changes in interest rates with a direct effect on fixed interest investments and an indirect effect on equity investments, changes in the conditions within particular industries, or a wide range of other factors.

It is a good plan for investors to review their investments at least every six months. Other reviews may be needed at times of any significant changes either in relation to the investor or to investment markets.

Base Reviews on Current Values

In reviewing investments, it is absolutely essential to work on the basis of current values. It is the present and future with which you are concerned, and not the past as reflected in the cost price that you happened to pay for an investment some time ago. For example, if you bought a stock many years ago at a price much lower than its current market value, it may be providing you a yield on your investment of 15 percent. But the yield which you have to consider in your review of investments is the yield which that investment offers on its current market value today. If that return together with a reasonable estimate of possible future capital gain is well below comparable figures for other stocks, then there would at least be a case for seriously considering selling that stock and investing elsewhere.

It is the present income yield and expectations of capital growth and/or perhaps increased income return in the future of various investments based on current market values which is the realistic standard.

Sensible Selling to Reduce Risk

An old investment saying well worth remembering is that eager sellers make good investors. This is not to suggest that frequent and reckless selling of investments is desirable—far from it. The point is that it is psychologically more difficult to make selling decisions than buying decisions, and it is easier for investors to constantly defer selling action that may be needed to improve investment results and reduce risks.

Remember that if you are considering stocks, you do not necessarily have to make a decision to sell all of your stocks or even all of your holdings of a particular stock. You can adopt the step system in selling a portion of your holding now and then watching the market closely for the timing of any further sales to take advantage of short-term swings. The following are examples of how selling can help in reducing risk and improving overall investment performance:

1. The sale or partial sale of investments that have risen rapidly in recent times, which could leave them vulnerable to significant decline when the market tides turned.
2. Selling to convert paper profits into realized gains, or maybe money into actual money.
3. Selling to cut losses when the market has not cooperated with your predictions.
4. Partial selling as a precaution when the overall market, the market for a particular stock, or business conditions in a particular company or industry raise some doubts as to the future.

As well as the positive aspects of selling outlined above, there is one particular trap which investors should avoid. It is the temptation whenever some investments must be sold to meet cash needs to sell the investments that are showing a good profit and retain those that have shown little gain or even a loss. If that practice is followed regularly, the portfolio can end up with all of the poorly performing stocks left in it and the good stocks eliminated through sales.

The Beta Approach to Risk

Part of modern portfolio theory taught at many educational institutions today involves the use of the "beta" in considering risks of stocks. Beta is a statistical measure designed to indicate whether a stock is more or less risky than the market as a whole. It is based on the covariance of the stock with the index representing the overall market. If the market were to increase by 10 percent, a stock with beta of 1 would also increase by 10 percent. A stock with a beta of 1.5 would increase by 15 percent, and a stock of 2 would increase by 20 percent. (Similar relative movements would be expected in the event of a market decline.)

Though this beta approach is popular in some investment circles, it has some serious weaknesses. One is that it relates only to the stock market and does not allow for the fact that the stock market itself is a medium to high risk investment area. Hence a stock with a beta of 1 could still be a relatively high risk investment compared to investments other than the stock market. The second disadvantage is that there is now some doubts as to whether the beta relationship between individual stocks and the whole market remains stable over time. There is a good deal of evidence to suggest that betas are not stable, and the fact that there was a certain relationship between stock market movements or overall investment returns of income and capital gain of a stock in the past will not necessarily apply in the future.

Summary of Part 3

Before proceeding in the next chapter to the third element of the three Rs of investing, relativity, a brief summary of Part 3 dealing with the question of risk could be helpful.

There can be investment risk in relation to both income and capital values. These risks include business risks, financial risk, information and accounting risk, and risk relating to changes in interest rates. Some of these risks, especially market risk and information risk, tend to be ignored in many investment discussions. It is also important to recognize that there can be high risk in what appear to be "good investments," including blue chip stocks.

Each investor needs to consider what is the appropriate risk category for him or her. This could range from very low risk for investors with limited funds for investments and limited earning capacity from other sources, to a very high risk policy at least for some of the portfolio for an investor with large amounts of capital and adequate income from other sources.

As far as the risk of various types of investments, which was discussed in Chapter 14, the range is from low risk investments such as short-term government loans and loans to companies with strong financial stature through medium-term fixed interest investments subject to some interest rate risk, longer-term fixed interest investments where the interest rate risk is greater, common stocks, income-producing property in the medium risk category, to high and very high risk investments including stock in speculative industries or new ventures, commodity markets, and futures trading.

Borrowing can help to improve investment results but does not increase risk, particularly where borrowings are significant in relation to the net worth of an investor and to his or her cash flow. That risk can be minimized by limiting total borrowings in relation to net worth and cash flow from other sources, matching long-term investments with medium- to long-term sources of funds, and seeing that there are adequate cash reserves from other sources.

It is necessary to control risk through measures such as the spread of investment, careful selection, and effective reviewing of portfolios at regular intervals. These reviews need to take into account changes in the situation of the investor as well as changes relating to the investment.

Appendix to Chapter 16: Sensitivity Analysis on Property Investment Proposition

The figures submitted by the seller of the property at a price of $200,000 of which the buyer would borrow $100,000 at 14 percent per annum give the following picture (amounts in thousands of dollars):

Gross revenue (fully let)	26.7
Less vacancies and/or rent concessions	0
Rental revenue	26.7
Less expenses	4.2
Net revenue before interest	22.5
Less interest (14 percent on $100,000)	14.0
Net earnings after interest	8.5
Net earnings as percentage of capital outlay	8.5%

Now let us do some sensitivity analysis by assuming changes in the crucial variables. Columns A, B, and C below allow for 7.5 percent, 10 percent, and 15 percent cost of vacancies and/or rent concessions, and increases of 43 percent, 57 percent, and 64 percent in expenses.

Columns B and C also allow for interest on borrowings increasing to 15 percent and 16 percent respectively.

	A	B	C
Gross revenue	26.7	26.7	26.7
Less vacancies and/or rent concessions	2.0	2.7	4.0
Rental revenue	24.7	24.0	22.7
Less expenses	6.0	6.6	6.9
Net revenue before interest	18.7	17.4	15.8
Less interest	14.0	15.0	16.0
Net earnings	4.7	2.4	(0.2 loss)
Net earnings as percentage of capital investment	4.7%	2.4%	(0.2% loss)

The net earnings figures above are markedly different from the figure of 8.5 percent on the basis of the figures supplied by the seller (even as the result of the relatively minor changes in column A). We could take the sensitivity analysis one stage further by considering the effect of an increase of 10 percent in construction costs assuming that further borrowed funds were not available, resulting in capital outlay being increased by $20,000 (i.e. 20 percent of planned outlay of $100,000).

The "bottom line" figure, that is, earnings as a percentage of capital outlay for the various situations outlined above, would then work out as follows:

Situation in Column A	3.9%
Situation in Column B	2.0%
Situation in Column C	(loss of 0.17%)

With the exception of the changes in expenses, the changes in the variables are not of major proportions. But the effect on the bottom line is most significant—especially in the latter figures above which allow for capital costs exceeding estimates (a situation which is by no means unusual) as well as for changes in revenue and expenses.

part 4

The Third R—
Relativity in Investing

17

The Need to Relate All Investments to Some Standard

When President Reagan invited to the White House the crew of *Australia II* after their win in the America's Cup Challange Series, he was not simply being gracious to visiting sportsmen from another country. He was recognizing the unusual feat of this crew in being the first challenger in 132 years to win the series. The win of the Australian crew, which caused wild enthusiasm at home and recognition throughout the world, was especially significant because it had not been achieved previously in the 132-year history of the America's Cup.

Most Facts Become Significant Relative to Some Standard

Most facts and figures become more significant when they are related to some standard. The statement that a large corporation made a profit of so many millions or billions does not mean much itself. It becomes significant when it is compared with a standard such as the profits achieved in the last few years, or profits as a percentage of net worth of the corporation.

An American used to reading weather reports where the temperature is recorded in degrees Fahrenheit and who is not familiar with the Celsius scale may think that it must be very cold in a foreign city where the temperature is recorded at 5°. That 5° Celsius is equivalent to 41° Fahrenheit, which is not an extremely low temperature. Only when he converts the Celsius figure into the Fahrenheit standard with which he is familiar do the figures become meaningful.

Relativity—the Third R of Investing

The average investor would fairly readily see the importance of the first two Rs of investing, return and risk. The significance of relativity in investments may not be so readily apparent. A little thought on the subject, however, shows that relativity must be an important factor in most investment decisions. Following are some examples of how relativity plays an important part in investment decisions:

1. *Return relative to risk.* If a certain return is available from low risk investment, then an investor would normally seek a higher return from investments offering a higher degree of risk.

2. *Primary profitability.* In considering an investment an investor may wish to compare the primary profitability, that is, the earnings of a company before interest and before taxation, with returns available on bonds or other investments.

3. *Return relative to inflation.* Returns on fixed interest investments of around 14 percent may have seemed very attractive a few years ago, but after allowing for an inflation rate of around 12 percent, the real return was far from attractive. A couple of years later when the interest rate was about 12 percent and the inflation rate 4 percent, the real return was considerably higher.

4. *Market ratings.* Within one particular market such as the stock market, prices of one stock may be compared with another on the basis of their dividend yield or price earnings multiple as an indication of the market rating. Often a better investment may be made in a stock with a relatively low market rating with good prospects rather than one with very good prospects but an already very high market rating, suggesting that future benefits have already been overanticipated.

5. *Return relative to interest rates.* Many years ago, when alternative investments such as bonds were offering about 4 percent, a dividend yield on common stocks of 5 percent indicated that stocks were attractively priced. The same dividend yield of 5 percent in the early 80s, when income returns of 12 percent were available from fixed interest investments, suggested that they were far from the bargain basement.

Those few examples are sufficient to illustrate the point that investment decisions are not made in a vacuum. Only by considering the principle of relativity can sound decisions be made.

Unsound Decisions If Relativity Is Ignored

If the principle of relativity is ignored, unsound investment decisions are likely to be made. How many billions have been invested in the U.S.

stock market in recent years, for example, on the basis that dividend yields and price earnings multiples are attractive compared with figures in earlier years when in fact they were far from attractive in relation to current interest rates and returns available from other investments?

It is a paradox that in the last two or three decades, when the amount of effort put into investment analysis expanded so greatly, the realities of the marketplace became more and more ignored. So much of the investment analysis was based on detailed studies of the earnings trend and future prospects of listed companies that investment recommendations became almost a system of reward for good performance or for management decisions by listed companies which put them in a situation where they could be expected to do well in the future.

The question of whether future benefits were already overanticipated in the market price tended to be ignored. Yet, for many investors the biggest single factor in the result of their equity investments is the difference between the price at which they buy and the price at which they sell. Over and over again, experience has shown that good results have been achieved by buying stocks with less than spectacular performance and future prospects at reasonable prices while losses have resulted from buying stocks with excellent performances and excellent prospects at seriously inflated prices.

18

The Principle of Relativity and the Opportunity Cost Concept

Probably the clearest illustration of the opportunity cost concept which I have seen occurred many years ago when I was a navigator in the Australian Air Force in World War II. An airman stationed on a base on the island of Noemfoor in what was then the Dutch East Indies told me he could not afford to drink the two bottles of beer which Australian servicemen were allowed to buy each week. That surprised me more than somewhat as the excise-free price of about 12 cents was very low—until he told me that the better paid U.S. troops in a neighboring camp loved Australian beer. They were offering $2 per bottle for it, and he could not afford to turn that opportunity down. The outlay cost per bottle for that serviceman was 12 cents, but the opportunity cost was the $2 available from potential purchasers which he would forego if he did not sell.

What Is Opportunity Cost?

Opportunity cost is the term used to describe a wider range of costs than those reported in the normal accounting system. Opportunity costs include costs of following a particular course of action compared with the cost of some alternative course. They may include savings that could be affected by an alternative course of action or the income that is foregone by not following an alternative course of action.

For a farmer, the opportunity costs of producing a particular crop could include the income foregone in producing some other crop or possibly using the land for raising livestock. For a manufacturer, the opportunity costs of producing a particular product or range of products would include the income foregone by not using resources in producing other products or in investing those resources in some other business.

Little Use in Investment Practice

The opportunity cost concept is widely used in business management. In conventional investment practice, many of the other techniques of the accountant are used in analyzing earnings and projecting them forward for future use. But the opportunity cost concept has been almost completely disregarded. If the opportunity cost concept were widely applied in investment practice, there would not have been so many unsound statements in recent years concerning yields available from the stock market. There would not have been enthusiastic statements about the stock market being very attractive because the dividend yields were higher and price earnings multiples lower than in earlier years.

Instead of those somewhat superficial statements, there would have been the more realistic statement that the opportunity cost of going into the stock market, or staying in it, was considerably greater than in earlier years (because dividend yield or earnings yield, which is the reciprocal of the price earnings multiple, has not been adjusted sufficiently to reflect the significant rise in interest rates, so the opportunity cost of equities was higher than in earlier years).

Some Examples of the Opportunity Cost Concept in Investment Decisions

The point was made in an earlier chapter that a large increase in the value of vacant land over a number of years may not necessarily mean a good investment result. When allowance is made for the fact that vacant land produces no cash inflow and involves an outflow in property taxes and other holding charges, the results may be far from spectacular. In terms of the opportunity cost concept, there is a significant opportunity cost in investing in vacant land or leaving funds in that investment in terms of the income foregone in other investments (the total of the positive income available in other investments plus the outflow on holding charges for the vacant land). A somewhat similar situation applies to low-yielding investments such as so-called blue chip stocks or stock bought at a time when they are popular and expectations are high.

At the other end of the investment scale, fixed interest may offer little or no prospect of significant capital gains. In that event, part of the opportunity cost of the fixed interest investment is the capital gain prospects that are foregone by going into, or staying in, that investment.

Opportunity Cost—the Key to Applying the Relativity Principle

From the comments above, you can see that opportunity cost provides a means of applying the principles of relativity in investments. By taking the opportunity cost into account, it is possible to make a more sensible decision on the relative merits of different types of investments.

For example, in considering a relatively low-yielding equity investment compared with a high-yielding fixed interest investment, the use of the opportunity cost concept provides a means of considering whether the expected capital gain will be adequate. We shall see in later chapters specifically how the capital gain target may be calculated. As this stage, it is sufficient to note that to be going into a low-yielding investment because it may produce some capital gain is not realistic. You would need to consider whether it would produce sufficient capital gain to compensate for the opportunity cost of that investment in terms of income foregone as well as other items such as transaction costs and additional risk, which are discussed in more detail later.

How to Calculate Relative Cost Figures

In considering the calculation of relative cost figures for investments, the first point to note is the obvious one that the figure to be calculated is a cost relative to some other investment. For example, a relative cost figure for equity investments such as common stocks could relate the cost of those investments to relatively low risk investments such as medium-term bonds.

The principle on which the calculation of relative costs is based is that of finding how much would have to be invested in an equity investment to produce the same income return as can be earned from the investment of $1 in fixed interest investments. This can be arrived at by dividing the interest rate on fixed interest investments by the dividend yield on common stocks. Hence, if the bond rate were 10 percent and the average dividend yield 5 percent, the relative cost figure for equities would be two. An investor would have to invest $2 in equities to obtain the same income return as that available for the investment of $1 in fixed interest investments.

Why Dividend Yields Are Used

For the last 20 years or so, most of the discussions among investment analysts relating to the income on common stocks have centered around earnings—either the price earnings multiple or the earnings yield, which is the reciprocal of the price earnings multiple expressed as a percentage. The earnings figure is normally highlighted on the argument that as part owners of the company, the purchasers of stock are buying an interest in total earnings—the undistributed earnings as well as the portion distributed.

Why, then, is what some would call the old-fashioned dividend yield figure used rather than the earnings figure? There are two reasons. The first is that dividend receipts are one of the two components of the overall return on equity investments (the other being the capital gain or loss arising from the difference between the price at which a stock is sold and that at which it is purchased). But the earnings yield, or more specifically the undistributed portion of the earnings yield, is not a component of investment return.

The argument that earnings yield is significant because stockholders have an equity in those undistributed earnings would only be valid if there was some way in which retained earnings were automatically reflected in stock prices. In fact they are not automatically reflected, and whether and to what extent a stockholder benefits from retained earnings depends on a whole host of factors. These include market cycles, changes in market fashions, the effect of changes in interest rates on market prices, and the inflow or outflow of foreign portfolio funds in a particular market—as well as the future earnings performance of the company. To put it another way, dividend yield relates to actual money, but earnings yield, including the undistributed portion, relates to maybe money.

The second reason for preferring dividend yield is that earnings figures tend to be unreliable because they can be affected by a wide range of different accounting treatments used by various companies or by one particular company in different periods. So changes in earnings yield may reflect changes in accounting treatment or the degree to which directors wish to portray a picture closer to what they would have liked to have happened rather than what actually happened.

Relative Cost for Other Equity Investments

The comments above relate to one particular type of equity, common stocks. The relative cost figure of common stocks can be more readily calculated because dividend yield figures and reliable price indexes are available for a period of many years. This information is not readily available for other investments, such as real estate. But the same principles could apply. It may be that in using the approach for other investments estimates may have to be made as to overall market movements. Certainly the concept of relative costs could be applied to one particular real estate investment where the actual or estimated return is readily available.

The Benefits of Using Relative Cost Figures

The benefits of using relative cost figures may be more apparent when the matter is discussed in more detail in later chapters. However, these benefits could be summarized at this stage as follows:

1. *An objective measure.* By relating the cost of equities to other investments under current conditions, it is an objective measure of cost which at least gives a first approximation as to whether particular investments are high or low priced rather than the traditional approach of thinking that stocks will rise because of improved earnings of companies, reduced interest rates, or other factors which may already have been overanticipated in the market.

2. *Comparison with other periods.* It means that an objective comparison may be made of the relative costs of equities in today's conditions with those in earlier years in deciding whether equity markets look attractive, thus avoiding the tendency to make unsound decisions by comparing dividend yields or price earnings multiples today with those prevailing in earlier years when returns from other investments were significantly different.

3. *Expectations and "blue sky".* In a way the relative cost figures at any particular time are a measure of expectations. If relative cost figures today are significantly higher than they were 20 years ago, this raises the question as to whether conditions for equities today are significantly better than they were in earlier years. If study suggests that they are not significantly more attractive, this would tend to be an indication that present prices may be inflated.

4. *Expected performance.* This is accomplished by measuring the results achieved in previous periods from investment at a time when the relative cost was the same as it is at present in assessing prospects of achieving capital gain. (Like many other measures this is subject to the doubt as to whether past experience is necessarily a good indicator of the future, but it is often better than using less objective methods.)

Some of the above points will be clearer in the discussions in succeeding chapter.

19

The Impact of Relative Costs on Stock Market Results

There is a widely held view that stock market prices, despite some fluctuations, produce good medium- to long-term results. The facts are different, with the actual results varying from very good to most disappointing. This can be seen from the following examples of price movements as measured by the Standard & Poor's Composite Index:

1. The person who invested in July 1982 just before the boom commenced would have enjoyed a price rise of 52.7 percent within the next 12 months—an increase many times greater than the amount needed to bridge the yield gap between the lower dividend yield and the higher return from bonds, and well above the returns from most other investments.

2. The investor who moved into the market at the low point in December 1974 had seen in July 1983 a substantial price rise of 11.2 percent per annum compound, another figure well above the figure needed to bridge the yield gap and provide a total return well above that for most other investments.

3. By contrast, for the person who invested at the end of 1968, market prices in July 1983 would have given him or her a gain of only 3.0 percent per annum.

4. In the previous 15 years from 1953 to 1968 prices increased by 10.5 percent per annum compound.

5. The figures in (3) and (4) above showing a long-term result in more recent years of less than one third that achieved in the preceding 15 years highlight the generally less favorable results since the mid-60s.

6. Since the mid-60s stock market investments, especially those made at times when prices are high in terms of dividend yields related to

bond yields, have generally failed to produce adequate and sustained medium-term gain.

Before turning to look at the impact of relative costs of medium-term results, it is well to consider the significance of that change.

The Significant Change since the Mid-60s

Today there is little truth in the claim that stock market investments generally provide sufficient capital gain to offset the effects of inflation and provide overall returns better than those available from fixed interest investments such as bonds (except for very successful short-term traders or those who are wise enough or lucky enough to buy at a low point in the market cycle and sell at a high point). But there was a substantial amount of truth in those statements in the period prior to the mid-60s. As far as the inflation hedge claim is concerned, the stock market has turned out to be pretty much like an umbrella on a fine day. In the period from the early 1950s to the early 60s when inflation was running about 1.5 percent per annum, stock markets produced gains of around 5 percent per annum. Some 20 years later between the early 70s and the early 80s, with inflation averaging about 8.4 percent per annum, the gain in the stock market was much lower than that figure. Indeed, in almost one in three of the five-year periods the stock market failed to produce any net increase in price.

Reasons for the Change

The primary reason for the change in conditions since the late 1960s is similar to that for any decline in a cyclical slump: that prices had reached unreasonable levels from which downward reaction was likely. In the 50s and early 60s stocks were low priced compared with other investments. In those days the immediate cash income by way of dividend yield was either greater than the bond yield or no more than about one third below that figure. By contrast, since the mid-60s the relative cost of stocks has been higher, with the dividend yield varying between about 40 and 60 percent of the bond yield. So in a sense the stock market had to run a lot harder to stay in the one spot in terms of just getting sufficient gain to break even with bonds.

As the period up to the mid-60s was generally a period of low interest rates, this made it relatively easy for companies to earn profits which were very attractive in relation to cost of money and to returns available elsewhere, as well as in relation to inflation. Since the mid-60s, interest rates have been high to very high compared with earlier years, making it more difficult for companies to earn at a rate which is attractive relative to cost of money, return on other investments, and the inflation rate.

Detailed Study of the Results to Clear Up Misconceptions

One of the reasons for the serious misconceptions about performance of the stock market is that many analyses are unsoundly based. For example, one booklet issued by an investment organization to support its claim that equity investments will always do better than other investments showed results for three periods up to the end of 1982, namely 57 years, 5 years, and 3 years. The gap between 57 and 5 years is quite significant, because comparisons for periods such as 10, 15, or 20 years would have shown significantly different results.

Another factor is that this particular study and others compare equity market results with those achieved by an investment in long-term bonds. But for the investor who wishes to avoid the higher risk of market fluctuation in common stocks, the alternative is not long-term bonds which themselves are subject to some risk of market fluctuation because of the effect of changes in interest rates. The person seeking to minimize risk would not go into long-term bonds but into bonds with three, four, or five years to maturity where the impact on capital value of any change in interest rates is minimized.

To overcome those serious weaknesses, the figures in this and the next chapter are based on a comprehensive study of 336 periods of five years each. The study commences with the period from January 1951 to January 1956 and concludes with the period from December 1978 to December 1983 (the last available five-year period when the study was completed). To illustrate the significant difference between results prior to and after the mid-60s, the figures have been analyzed for two periods of 14 years: 1951 to 1964, inclusive, and 1965 to 1978, inclusive.

The average (arithmetic mean) of the five-year gain in prices over the 168 periods of five years in each of those two periods was as follows:

> 1951–1964   10.9% per annum
> 1965–1978   0.9% per annum

The median or middle of the range figure was as follows:

> 1951–1964   8.4% per annum
> 1965–1978   0.7% per annum

The Use of Five-Year Periods

One reason for the use of the five-year period is that it provides a comparison with a medium-term bond, which would be the alternative for most investors wishing to avoid the higher risk of market fluctuation in common stocks. Another reason is that in the stock market five years is a long enough period to smooth out what would otherwise be the distorting effect of sharp upward or downward swings in prices.

Losses over Five-Year Periods

Set out below are the figures for the two periods showing the number of periods in which the five-year result was a net decline in price and the percentage of that figure to the total of 168 periods:

Period	Number	Percentage of Total
1951–1964	0	0%
1965–1978	51	30

The fact that in the period prior to the end of 1964 there were no five-year periods in which a net decline occurred and that after 1964 a net decline occurred in 30 percent of the cases is most significant.

Relative Costs over the 28 Years

The point has already been made that in the earlier periods the relative cost of stocks (bond yield divided by average dividend yield) was generally much lower than in the period after 1964. The full extent of this can be seen from the figures below:

Date	Interest Rate	Dividend Yield	Relative Cost
January 1951	2.71	6.34	0.43
January 1961	4.48	3.28	1.37
January 1973	7.37	2.69	2.74
December 1974	9.03	5.43	1.66
February 1983	12.76	4.21	3.03

Though these figures would fluctuate according to both changes in interest rates and, more particularly, cyclical movements in stock prices, the general trend has been upward from the low point of 0.43 in January 1951 to the high of 2.74 in January 1973. In December 1974, when the stock market was at its lowest point for many years, the relative cost declined to 1.66. Since then there has been a generally upward movement with some fluctuations. In February 1983, at a date after the end of the period of five years covered by the survey (but relevant for present considerations), the relative cost was a very high figure of 3.03.

Relative Cost at Time of Investment and Five-Year Results

So far we have seen that over the years stock market results have varied from very good to very disappointing, and the results since the mid-60s have generally been much lower than in the preceding period. We have also seen that relative costs have generally risen significantly over the last 25 to 30 years.

Logic would suggest that, generally speaking, results in the long term should be better if investment is made at a time of low relative costs compared with investments made when relative costs are higher. If relative costs go higher, there is an indication that the market may be overanticipating. To some extent, the gap between the dividend yield and the returns available elsewhere may be seen as a sort of realism gap. Though some of that gap could well be filled by capital gain, it is also probable that a large gap could represent a substantial amount of overanticipation or "blue sky" in stock market prices.

This belief can be tested by checking the actual results achieved over various five-year periods and the relative cost at the commencement of those periods. Because of the significant difference between the results after 1965 and prior to that time, the figures below are based on the second half of the overall survey, that is, the 168 periods of five years each commencing with January 1965 to January 1970 and ending with December 1978 to December 1983. If the earlier figures were included, the significance of relative costs in relation to investment results would be of even larger proportions than those reflected below. However, as there has been a significant change in investment conditions since the mid-60s, it is better to relate to figures for the period since 1965.

A study of these figures over many years indicated in broad terms the relationship was as follows:

Relative Cost at Time of Investment	Five-Year Investment Results
Under 2.0	Reasonably good
2.0 to 2.39	Disappointing
2.40 and above	Very disappointing

For those who may prefer to visualize it in another way, the first category of relative cost under 2.0 corresponds to dividend yield being at least half of the bond yield. The second category corresponds to a dividend yield of between about 0.4 and 0.5 of bond yield, and the third category to a dividend yield of less than about 0.4 of bond yield.

The point has already been made that except for a minority of short-term traders and those who were wise enough or lucky enough to buy at a low point in the cycle and sell at a high point, overall stock market results have been a good deal less favorable than has been commonly believed. Hence, the terms above in the second column have to be seen within that context. A cynic, for example, may say that the term "reasonably good" for the first category could be replaced by the term "less disappointing."

Overall Result

On the basis of the 168 periods, the average (arithmetic mean) gain or loss over the five-year periods on investments made in various relative cost categories were as follows:

Relative Cost	Annual Gain or Loss
Under 2	4.8% per annum
2.0 to 2.39	2.9% per annum
2.4 and above	Loss of 0.4% per annum

Please note that these annual gain or loss figures relate only to the component of overall return coming from an increase or decrease in prices. They do not take into account the dividend income, which is discussed below.

The tendency for high relative cost to produce less favorable results can also be seen by looking at the median (middle of the range) figures. These figures are 3.6 percent, 1.1 percent, and a loss of 1.1 percent per annum respectively.

Success Rate in Achieving Any Gain in Price

An analysis of the figures shows the following situation in relation to the achievement of any gain from an increase in price over the five-year periods. The success rate is the number of periods expressed as a percentage of the total number of periods in each category. (Of the total of 168 periods, the relative cost was under 2.0 in 69 periods, between 2.0 and 2.39 in 63 periods, and 2.4 or above in 36 periods.)

Relative Cost	Success Rate in Achieving Any Gain
Under 2.0	87%
2.0 to 2.39	62%
2.4 and above	39%

If you were to look at these figures from the viewpoint of downside risk of incurring a loss of capital, the figures would range from a fairly low 13 percent for relative cost of under 2, 38 percent for cost of 2.0 to 2.39, and 61 percent for the high relative cost category.

Achievement of Enough Gain to Equal Five-Year Bonds

The next step was to analyze the success rate as a percentage of periods in each relative cost category in achieving enough gain just to break even with five-year bonds after allowing for income tax and capital gains tax (details of the calculations are set out in the next chapter). The results are as follows:

Relative Cost	Success Rate in Breaking Even with Bonds
Under 2.0	67%
2.0 to 2.39	11%
2.4 and above	11%

Achievement of Additional Gain to Compensate for Risk

Investors in common stocks are exposed to significant market risk, even if they select their stocks carefully and attempt to minimize risk by spreading funds over a number of different investments. Investors in bonds, if they avoid longer term bonds by concentrating on terms of no more than about five years to maturity where the impact of changes in interest rates on capital value is minimized and select their bonds carefully, face relatively low risk. The big difference is that there is a contractual obligation for the borrower to repay the funds on maturity, while the stock market investor is dependent entirely on the fluctuating situation of the market when he or she chooses to sell or has to sell.

Because of the greater risk, common stocks would need to provide a higher return than lower risk bonds. So it would be necessary to multiply the bond return by a figure to compensate for that higher risk. What that figure would be is a matter for judgment. As it is possible to increase return on fixed interest investments by $\frac{1}{10}$ or more without sacrificing too much safety or taking much additional risk, it would seem that because of the higher market risk in common stocks, the multiple should be about 1.5, that is, the target return for higher risk equities should be 1.5 times the return available from fixed interest investments such as medium-term (five-year) bonds (after allowing for income tax and capital gains tax). Details of the calculation and some simplifications in the interests of clarity are discussed in the next chapter.

As a percentage of the total of 69, 63, and 36 periods in the three relative cost categories, the success rate in achieving total return equal to 1.5 times the five-year return from a bond investment (or better) is as follows:

Relative Cost	Success Rate
Under 2.0	56%
2.0 to 2.39	11%
2.4 and above	11%

Validity of the Survey Results

As both the overall results of stock market investments and the results analyzed according to relative cost at time of investment differ very greatly from the common perception of how the stock market behaves, a comment on its validity would be appropriate. First, it is based on results as measured by the Standard & Poor's Composite Index of 500 stocks, which is a more reliable indicator of overall market movements than some other indexes that are based on a much smaller number of stocks. Second, the overall results are based on a total of 336 periods of five years each, and the results for the latter half of the total period—from January 1965 to December 1978—are based on 168 periods of five years each. That is a large enough number to ensure that the survey is free from the possible distortion that could occur with a smaller number of observations.

The figures used in the results analyzed according to relative cost at time of investment are based on 68 observations for relative cost under 2, 63 observations for relative cost between 2 and 2.39, and 36 observations for relative cost of 2.4 and above. Another most important point is that in comparing stock market results with other investments, the comparison is made with the type of investment which would be made by a prudent investor who wished to avoid the higher risk associated with fluctuations in the stock market—that is, medium-term bonds of no more than five years to maturity—so that the effect of any changes in interest rates on capital values would be minimized.

The latter point is most important, because many comparisons of investment results and arguments in support of the efficient markets hypothesis are invalid because they compare stock market results either with very short-term investments with one month to maturity at low interest rates, or with long-term bonds which can be in the medium risk category because of the effect of changing interest rates rather than low risk medium-term bonds.

Finally, the period of five years used in measuring the results is long enough to overcome the distortion on results for shorter periods of the sharp short-term movements. (The five-year period is about one third longer than the average length of stock market cycles.)

Lessons from the Survey Results

Apart from the basic point that stock market results are a good deal less favorable than the common perception of what has happened in the market, the figures in relation to relative costs are extremely interesting. The mean loss of 0.4 percent per annum and median loss of 1.1 percent per annum for investments made at relative costs of 2.4 and above contrasted with gains of 4.8 percent and 3.6 respectively when relative costs at time of investment were under 2 cannot be ignored.

To the extent that past experience may be a guide to the future (though it may not necessarily be), the success rate of only 39 percent in achieving any increase in price over a five-year period (with 61 percent of the periods producing a loss) for investment made at a relative cost of 2.4 and above contrasts markedly with the 87 percent success rate (a loss in only 13 percent of the periods) when the relative cost was under 2.

In terms of achieving enough gain to equal the result from an investment in five-year bonds, the success rate of 67 percent for investment at relative costs of under 2 is over six times the success rate of 11 percent for investment at relative costs of 2.4 and above. Similar contrast emerges in the figures for achieving enough gain to provide a total return 1.5 times that available from medium-term bonds. On this standard the success rate for investment at relative costs of under 2 was 56 percent compared with 11 percent when relative cost was 2.4 and above.

In summary, this means that investment when the relative cost was under 2 may not necessarily produce spectacular results, but by comparison with investment at other times the results are relatively good. This suggests that investors can go into the stock market or stay in it with confidence when relative costs are at those levels. In the intermediate category of relative costs of 2 to 2.39, the results are disappointing in relation to the target of breaking even with a medium-term bond investment or reaching the higher standard of a total return 1.5 times the bond return to compensate for higher risk.

So there is a fairly strong argument for not moving into the market and for moving out or at least reducing total market holdings when relative costs are in the highest category.

As for the third category of relative costs above 2.4, the results are so disappointing in relation to all three standards that investors should refrain from moving into the market and move almost completely out of it once relative costs are in that area. Naturally, the comments relate to the medium-term investor. It is possible that a minority of short-term traders may make profits by buying stocks when relative costs are high if they are wise enough or lucky enough to take advantage of short-term swings either for the market overall or for some particular stocks in areas which are enjoying wide popularity, such as high technology stocks in late 1982 (prior to their very serious reaction a little later). But this type of investment is intrinsically a higher risk operation and is generally not suitable for the typical investor.

20

Assessing Prospects of Achieving Adequate Market Gain

As the return from a stock market investment is comprised of the actual money of dividend receipts and the maybe money of capital gain, it is necessary to assess the prospects of achieving adequate gain. In doing so, it would be wise to consider the two significant lessons that emerge from the last chapter. These are that sustained capital gain (as distinct from temporary gain followed by a decline) is a good deal less than is commonly believed and that relative cost at time of investment has had a significant effect on investment results.

Though past experience may not necessarily be a good guide to what will happen in the future, it is a factor which should not be ignored. At times of high relative cost, an investor would need to be very careful indeed to ensure that future prospects either for the market overall or for a particular stock are so exceptionally favorable that results could differ greatly from that suggested by past experience.

In applying the lessons of the past to these decisions, two steps are involved:

1. Calculate the amount of capital gain to achieve the particular target, whether it be the avoidance of any capital loss, enough capital gain just to break even with medium-term bonds (after allowing for income tax and capital gains tax), or a larger amount to bring the total return from common stocks up to a figure greater than the return from bonds to compensate for the higher risk (perhaps to a figure 1.5 times the bond return).
2. Check the success rate in the past of the stock market in producing that required amount of capital gain or better over a five-year period for investments in various relative cost categories.

Success Rate in Achieving Various Levels of Capital Gain

The table below shows the success rate of the stock market at various levels of relative cost in achieving capital gain. The figures in the second, third, and fourth columns show the success rate for the various relative cost categories in achieving *at least* the amount of capital gain in the first column.

Required Gain (percent per annum)	Success Rate in Achieving at Various Levels of Relative Cost		
	Under 2	2 to 2.39	2.40 and Above
0	87%	59%	39%
2	86	41	11
4	44	25	9
6	31	7	7
8	24	5	0
10	13	0	0
12	0	0	0

Calculation of Capital Gain Required to Break Even with Bonds

In this calculation and the subsequent calculations of the amount of gain required to produce a larger return to compensate for the risk, certain details have been omitted to avoid complicating the calculations, as tests show they would not materially affect the figures. For example, the calculations assume that the interest receipts on bond investment and dividend receipts on share investments would be reinvested at the same rate as that which applied when the investment was made. In fact the rates would vary depending on interest rate changes and stock market movements. The costs of buying and selling, such as brokerage, have not been taken into account. The figures have not been adjusted to allow for the fact that capital gains tax would be paid only when the stocks were sold, so that the benefit of not having to pay that tax until later is not reflected in the figures.

As far as taxation is concerned, the calculations are based on an estimated total of federal and state income tax of 40 percent and capital gains tax of 20 percent.

Because there is a tendency for dividend payments to grow somewhat, the dividend yield at time of investment has been multiplied by 1.1.

The first step is to calculate the total after-tax return from bonds, assuming, as indicated above, that interest receipts would be reinvested at the rate applicable at the time of the original investment. This is calculated as follows:

$$X = (1 + ((1-T1) \times I/100))^5 - 1$$

where X is the five-year earnings from bond investments after tax, $T1$ is the total federal and state income tax estimated at 40 percent or 0.4, and I is the bond yield percent (which is divided by 100 to convert it to decimal figures).

The next step is to calculate the amount of the total required gain which would be obtained from the dividend component of investment in common stocks. This is calculated as follows:

$$Y = (1 + ((1 - T1) \times (1+K) \times D/100))^5 - 1$$

where Y is the portion of overall stock market earnings to come from dividends, K is the factor to allow for growth in dividends (we assume this factor to be 0.1), and D is the dividend yield percent divided by 100 to express it in decimal form.

The first calculation gives the total required return to equal the return from bonds, and the second calculation gives the amount of total earnings which can be expected from dividends. The remaining step is to arrive at the portion of total required return from common stocks which would have to come from capital gain by deducting earnings from dividends from total required earnings, with due allowance for capital gains tax. This is calculated as follows:

$$Z = (\sqrt[5]{1 + ((X - Y)/(1 - T2))} - 1) \times 100$$

where Z is the required capital gain from common stock investments, X and Y are as calculated above, and $T2$ is the capital gains tax (estimated to be 20 percent or 0.2) with the result being multiplied by 100 to express it in percentage figures.

Required Capital Gain to Compensate for Higher Risk

The point has been made that because of the higher risk, especially risk of market fluctuation in common stocks, the total return from that investment including both dividends and capital gain should be significantly higher than the return available from lower risk medium-term fixed interest investments (remember that if the period to maturity of fixed interest investments is limited to no more than five years, the effect of any subsequent changes in interest rates on capital value is minimized). Hence, the first element in the calculation above would need to be multiplied by a factor to allow for the need for common stocks to produce a greater overall return. For reasons outlined in the last chapter, it would seem reasonable to aim for a return from common stocks equal to 1.5 times the return from low risk medium-term bonds.

If that multiple is considered appropriate, then the steps in calculating the required capital gain to meet that target would be as follows:

1. Multiply X as calculated above by 1.5 (or whatever other multiple a particular investor may consider appropriate).
2. Calculate Y and Z as set out above.

Assessing Prospects of Achieving Required Capital Gain

Having calculated the amount of capital gain required either to break even with fixed interest investments or to provide a larger return to compensate for the higher risk of equity investments such as common stocks, the next step is to see what the success rate was in the past in achieving at least that amount of capital gain. This is done by referring to the table earlier in the chapter (p. 118), using the figure in the column for the relative cost category in which the current relative cost figure at time of investment is located. For example, if the relative cost were 2.25, it would be the middle relative cost category, the third column in the table, that is relevant.

By running down the first column to the row for the required capital gain percentage per annum and across to the column for the relevant cost category, the success rate can be ascertained. For example, with a relative cost figure of 2.25 and required capital gain of 6 percent per annum the figure in the fourth row and third column gives the success rate of 7 percent.

Subject to the point made earlier that past experience may not necessarily be a good guide to the future, the success rate in achieving the gain needed to meet a particular target can be a most useful indicator. If the success rate is low, then an investor going into the stock market at that time would need to be very careful to ensure that his or her buying decision is based on a thorough and objective examination and not simply a matter of being carried on by the enthusiasm of the moment. It is well to remember that widespread enthusiasm for the market tends to coincide with high prices just before a decline commences—for example, the spring of 1983, early 1973, or mid-1976.

21

Relative Costs and the Situation in the First Quarter of 1984

As an example of how the approach outlined in preceding chapters can be applied in practice, we could consider the situation in the first quarter of 1984.

Relative Costs

For much of that period the bond yield (Moody's Aa) was around 12.75 and the dividend yield around 4.20. Thus the relative cost was 3.04 (12.75 divided by 4.20). That is a very high relative cost figure. It is not only in the top range, the 2.40 and above, for which the table in the preceding chapter shows very disappointing results, but it is about the highest relative cost figure for several decades. It contrasts with relative cost figures of less than 0.5 30 years ago and 1.66 in December 1974 at the low point of that cycle. It is also more than 10 percent higher than the figure of 2.74 in January 1973 at the peak of that cycle.

All this means that despite the decline of around 10 to 12 percent in prices from the 1983 peak, the stock market in the first quarter of 1984 could hardly be described as the greatest bargain since the Louisiana Purchase.

Required Gain to Break Even with Bonds

On the basis of the formula for the calculations set out in the last chapter, the figure would be as follows:

X (5-year after-tax return from bonds) $= 0.446$
Y (after-tax return from dividends over 5 years) $= 0.147$
Net (after-tax capital gain) $X - Y$ $= 0.299$
$Z = \left(\sqrt[5]{1 + (0.299/0.8)} - 1\right) \times 100$ $= 6.6\%$ per annum

Success Rate in Achieving Required Gain

A reference to the table in the previous chapter and to the more detailed figures on which it is based shows that the highest capital gain per cent per annum over a five-year period achieved when the relative cost was 2.4 and above is just below the figure of 6.6 percent per annum required capital gain. Hence, the success rate would be zero.

This means that, on the basis of past experience, stock prices were so high relative to other investments in the first quarter of 1984 that there has been no occasion in the past from the periods surveyed in which the market produced the amount of gain that is required just to break even with bonds. So for the medium-term investor the stock market would appear to be far from attractive.

Incidentally, calculations along this line in the spring of 1983 would have indicated that the market was far from attractive at a time when most commentators were suggesting that further substantial rises were likely.

Unless there was evidence to suggest that economic conditions and trends for corporate profits were considerably better in the first quarter of 1984 than in the past, going into the market or staying substantially in the stock market at that stage would be unwise. There would be a good case for those already in the market to consider a substantial reduction of their holdings.

This does not necessarily mean that the market will not rise. If there is enough enthusiasm, much of it fostered by those who find it profitable to promote the idea of stock market investment without bothering to point out that on an objective basis stocks are very highly priced, there could be short-term rises from which alert traders may benefit. Past experience would certainly suggest that the market in early 1984 was at dangerously high levels. If there were to be a rise in prices in 1984 or 1985 or even later, that would not invalidate the above comments. Remember, we are talking of five-year gain, and what the figures of the past suggest is that the market early in 1989 is unlikely to be 37.4 percent above its early 1984 levels to provide the 6.6 percent per annum capital gain (after allowing for capital gains tax) that would be needed just to break even with bonds.

As the figures suggest that the past success rate in achieving sufficient gain just to break even with bonds is about zero, the prospects of enough capital gain to provide a total return 1.5 times that of bonds would be extremely dim. If the interest earnings to 0.446 were multiplied by 1.5, this would work out at 0.669. Deducting the dividend component of the earnings of 0.147, this would leave a required after-tax capital gains figure of 0.512. Allowing for a capital gains tax of 20 percent or 0.2, this would mean a total gain of 0.64. That would be equivalent to 10.4 percent per annum—an amount of gain for which the success rate from the large number of periods in the survey was zero not only when relative cost was 2.4 and above, but when it was 2 to 2.39. Indeed, even when the relative cost was under 2 the success rate in achieving more than 10 percent per annum capital gain was only 13 percent, or about one in eight times.

In summary, on the objective basis of relative costs which relates the stock market with other investments currently available (rather than with price earnings multiples or dividend yields many years ago when earnings available on alternative investments were much lower), the stock market in the first quarter of 1984 was far from the bargain basement. Past experience certainly indicates that for the next five years bonds were likely to do better than common stocks for investors (with the possible exception of some very astute short-term traders).

Commentators who were suggesting that the stock market was attractive because prices were lower than 6 to 12 months earlier were ignoring the lessons of the past and the total abstainer analogy—just as a person who reduces his drinking from three bottles of liquor a day to two does not qualify as a total abstainer, so a decline from a very high level to a slightly lower level does not make the stock market a bargain. That is especially so in the 1984 situation when in terms of dividend yield (the actual money component of common stock return) the reduction in stock prices had been offset by increased interest rates to bring relative costs up to higher levels.

22

The Need to See Relativity and Relative Cost Figures in Correct Perspective

"My mind is made up—don't confuse me with the facts." That sort of attitude is widespread in the investment world. Those selling one particular type of investment, or institutions, specialists, or analysts who have fallen in love with one type of investment, have developed a great ability to ignore relevant facts. All sorts of approaches are advertised as providing a simple, magical way of achieving great investment success. (A cynic has said that a person who writes books about how to make money on the stock market is a person who has lost everything on the stock market except his typewriter or perhaps, today, his word processor.)

The principle of relativity and the use of relative costs as well as a means of calculating capital gain targets, assessing the prospects of achieving those targets, and other matters discussed in the last few chapters, all make a useful contribution to sound investment practice. But they don't pretend to be a magical approach which ensures immediate investment success. There is still truth in the old saying that nobody rings a bell at the top or bottom of the market, and it is only when we look back later with the benefit of that wonderful analytical tool of hindsight that we know for sure that a certain point was the peak or the trough.

The principle of relativity and the other matters referred to above do not pretend to be the bell that tells you automatically to the day or the hour when to move into the market or when to move out of it. So, it is important to recognize what these measures can do and what they cannot do before going on to discuss investment policy and strategy and particular types of investments.

What the Principle of Relativity Can Do

The principle of relativity, along with the investment measures derived from it, can provide many useful benefits, including the following:

1. A more objective and logical approach than the traditional investment approach to decisions whether to move into equity markets, stay in them, or increase or reduce holdings in those markets.
2. It highlights actual achievement of equity markets in the past as distinct from popular misconception based on widespread promotion of fallacies such as you can't go wrong in blue chips, good stocks keep pace with inflation, property values never go down.
3. It provides a means of setting targets for capital gain on an objective basis that makes allowance for the extra risk involved in equity investments, especially market risk.
4. It provides a measure of the expectations or possible "blue sky" in share market prices at any particular time. With expectations being much higher now than at some time in the past, the investor can proceed to assess whether that higher expectation is justified on the basis of prospects for the economy for a particular industry, for corporate profits, or for any particular investment sectors compared with prospects in the past.
5. It provides an objective means of comparing the price of equity investments with other investments in current conditions of earning capacity and interest rates rather than the traditional approach of comparing prices on the basis of dividend yields or price earnings multiples with previous periods when interest rates and other conditions were markedly different.
6. It provides a measure of the extent to which equity prices have drifted away from price related to earning capacity and current interest rates as an indicator of potential significant decline if and when the market returns to a more realistic assessment.

What the Principle of Relativity Does Not Do

Investors should realize that the principle of relativity, along with other measures derived from it, cannot do the following:

1. Give an absolute indication of the point at which a market is going to reach a peak or trough. (A high relative cost indicates that the market is high, but temporary enthusiasm, effective selling of equity investments, or market moods or fashions could cause the market to rise to even higher levels of relative cost.)

2. Be a useful guide to short-term trading. For reasons outlined above, the short-term trader has to be more aware of the mood of the market rather than an objective assessment based on relative costs or other standards.
3. It cannot eliminate investment risk, though it may be useful in indicating times when risk may be higher.

Investors who recognize both the benefits of the principle of relativity and its limitations find it a real help in making their investment decisions. Those who understand these matters would certainly not be tempted to think of this principle or the use of relative costs or the Expectation Index as any single magical rule that will produce instant investment success.

The Efficient Markets Fallacy

This theory is popular in some educational institutions and some sections of the investment business. According to this theory, as information about corporate earnings, economic trends, interest rates, and other matters is readily available and widely published, market prices at any time are a reasonable indication of the value of the particular stock or the market overall. There is a fairly large body of literature supporting the theory, a good deal of which is superficially attractive. A closer examination shows that the arguments in support of the efficient market fallacy are based on unrealistic simplifying assumptions. One assumption used is that decisions are made on information. If all investment decisions were made by computers without any element of human judgment, there could be some truth in that statement. The facts are that investment decisions are made by human beings, and it is their *perception* of the information which has a big bearing on their decisions. That perception is often affected by the mood of the moment.

The theory also overlooks the herd instinct among institutional investors in which they seem to be rushing into the market or rushing out of it in buying or selling panics. The principle of relativity, relative costs, and the expectations referred to in earlier chapters show that the market is far from efficient. A good deal of its fluctuations are due to changes in the mood of the moment, the more or less regular cyclical pattern, and other factors quite apart from the information which the efficient market fallacy tends to consider is the only factor involved.

In a sense, relative costs give some indication of the degree of inefficiency in the market. For example, the information I quoted in a television interview in May 1983 to the effect that on the basis of past experience, investors then going into the stock market had only about 1 chance in 16 (on the basis of the Dow Jones Industrial Average) of doing as well in common stocks as they would by investing in bonds was a reminder that the market had reached somewhat inflated levels because of the speculative excesses of the previous six months.

Summary of Part 4

It is now time to briefly summarize Part 4, dealing with the third R of investing, relativity. This part commenced with a reminder that in investments, as indeed in most other matters, it is necessary to relate figures to some standard before they become meaningful. The opportunity cost concept, which is widely used in business management but generally ignored in investments, provides a means of applying the relativity principle. For equity investments, the opportunity costs are comprised of three elements—the income foregone, the costs of buying and selling, and the additional risk, especially market risk, compared with other investments.

Relative cost is defined as the amount which has to be invested in equity investments to produce the same income as can be obtained from the investment of one dollar in fixed interest investments. It is calculated by dividing the interest rate on bonds by the average dividend yield. In the stock market, relative costs range from around 1.2 in the early to mid-60s to over 3.0 in the early 80s. There has been a trend toward higher relative costs in the late 70s and early 80s, primarily because equity markets did not adjust to considerable increases in interest rates.

The figures discussed in Chapter 20 reveal facts very different from popular misconceptions. First, the overall performance of the stock market has been disappointing. Its record is poor in relation to achieving enough capital gain to bridge the yield gap, cover transaction costs, and produce a total return 1.5 times that available from lower risk investments to compensate for the higher risk (especially market risk). The figures also show a significant difference between the price movements over a five-year period from investments made at times of low and high relative costs. In Chapter 21, there is a table showing the prospects of achieving the required capital gain on the basis of past experience over a survey of 65 periods of five years each. From this it may be possible to indicate the degree of expectation or perhaps "blue sky" in the market.

The principle of relativity, relative costs figures, and benefits derived from the application of the opportunity cost concept are useful investment tools but not a magic formula for investment success. One significant factor revealed by consideration of relative costs is the extent to which equity markets in recent times have differed from the realities of earning capacity and current interest rates. This would mean that markets could be exposed to substantial loss if, at some time in the future, they were to return to more realistic prices relating to those standards.

part 5

Practical Aspects
of Day-by-Day
Investment Decisions

23

The Need for Investment Policy and Strategy

Unless investors seriously consider the need for an appropriate investment policy and strategy, they may end up like the businessman who said, "Ours is a nonprofit organization," and then ruefully added, "We didn't plan it that way—that's just how it worked out." Many of the portfolios I have reviewed over the years have been concentrated in relatively high risk investments. This was not because of a conscious decision by investors to adopt a high risk policy. Rather, it was due to the fact that they had not bothered to formulate any definite investment policy and simply went into those investments which happened to be popular at the time when they had funds to invest.

Before investors start to think about whether to buy this investment or that investment, they need to work out, perhaps with the help of an investment adviser, the basic investment policy they should be adopting and a suitable investment strategy for putting that policy into effect.

Investment Policy

Most investors are familiar with the use of the word *policy* in relation to governments, business corporations, or other organizations. For the investor, policy involves the same basic constituent, that is, a settled or definite course or method.

If the investors referred to in earlier paragraphs had adopted a definite policy of a more balanced portfolio with limited investment in high risk stocks, they would not have ended up with the portfolio unduly concentrated in that area. To put it another way, their failure to adopt a definite policy in effect led them, be default, into following a policy of high risk investments without question.

Investment policy in the first instance involves a consideration of whether the investor should follow an extremely conservative policy, an extremely venturesome policy, or a policy somewhere in between those two extremes. Having made that basic decision, the investor can then proceed to think in terms of degree of risk exposure, the approximate proportion of capital to be invested in various areas, and other relevant questions, including the preference for short-, medium-, or long-term investments.

Ideally, a policy should be definite enough to provide the basis for making investment decisions within a coherent framework but flexible enough to cope with changing conditions. For that reason, the policy may involve setting minimum and maximum limits for the percentage of the portfolio in various types of investments. For example, on the basis of various factors discussed in earlier chapters dealing with risk of investments and the risk exposure for different types of investors, a particular investor may decide that he or she should have a minimum of 25 percent of his/her portfolio in low risk investments. That portion could then serve as the sheet anchor to ensure that the adverse effects of any sudden market reverse, if he or she does not move out of it in time, do not have as serious an effect as would otherwise be the case.

Having set a minimum of 25 percent, he or she may then consider that because it is appropriate for him/her to have some funds invested in equity investments capable of producing capital gain with possible tax benefits, the proportion in the low risk investments should not exceed, say, 60 percent. In that event, his/her policy would include a percentage investment in low risk, short- to medium-term fixed interest investments of between 25 and 60 percent. The decision on what is the appropriate percentage at any time is a matter discussed later in the chapter under the heading of investment strategy.

In setting investment policy, it is important to consider the various characteristics of different types of investments. For example, it is not good enough simply to say that X percent will go into fixed interest investments. Remember the point made in earlier chapters that in longer term fixed interest investments, the risk of adverse effect on capital in the event of subsequent change in interest rates is greater than in investment in short- to medium-term fixed interest investments. So, the policy should be specific enough to allow for differences of that type.

For some investors, it may be necessary to make a policy decision that no investment at all should be made in certain areas. For example, investors with very limited capital and very low income from other sources or unreliable income from other sources may have to include in their policy little or no investment in higher risk areas such as commodities, futures trading, or more volatile stocks. For such an investor it may also be necessary to think in terms of a policy limit of perhaps 10 to 20 percent, even in favorable conditions, on medium risk investments such as common stocks, income-producing property, etc.

Investment Strategy

Investment policy deals basically with the internal situation of a particular investor. Investment strategy is concerned with the external realities of the marketplace. Having set a sound policy, the investor needs to look at the market realities to decide whether or to what extent the investment policy should be modified because of present realities in the marketplace.

Investment strategy may involve considering what level within the minimum and maximum percentage of the total portfolio set out in the policy for a particular investment is appropriate under present investment conditions. For example, if policy considerations are that common stock investments should constitute between 20 and 50 percent of the total portfolio, then a percentage closer to 20 percent would be appropriate at times of high relative cost, with the market at a situation where prices have already risen considerably and a reaction or cyclical downturn appears imminent, or where prospects for the economy or for corporate earnings are becoming unfavorable. On the other hand, in the reverse situation of fairly low relative costs, with the market showing some signs of recovery after a significant decline and favorable economic or corporate earnings prospects, investment strategy could involve going closer to the higher limit in the policy prescriptions for that type of investment.

Influences Affecting Investment Policy

To a considerable extent, the influences that affect considerations on investment policy are tied up with the degree of risk to which the capital can be exposed. These matters were discussed in some detail in Part 3 of this text.

Obviously, the person with a large amount of capital, with high or assured income from a profession, business, or other source, with many years of working life ahead of him or her, could afford to adopt a more venturesome policy (a greater percentage of the portfolio in medium and high risk investments) than the person with a limited amount of capital and low or unreliable income from other sources, who is retired or close to retirement with little or no working life ahead of him/her to rebuild any capital losses from adverse investment experience out of subsequent earnings.

Influences on Investment Strategy

Turning to the external realities of the marketplace and the extent to which these will warrant some modifications of the investment policy, the following are the factors which need to be considered:

1. The relative cost of equity investment, because the figures discussed in Part 4 indicate lower prospects of good results from investment at high relative cost.
2. Cyclical position of the market and the possibility of a significant cyclical slump being imminent.
3. Overall economic trends and prospects for corporate earnings.
4. Interest rate trends (as a decline in interest rates could be good for equity investments except to the extent to which any likely decline has already been anticipated or overanticipated by the market) and vice versa.
5. The momentum of the market indicated by measures such as the Coppock Indicator of possible turning points (on the basis that a market which has developed an upward movement may maintain that momentum for some time even if fundamental indicators may suggest that the market is overpriced).
6. Investment in a particular foreign market. Inflow from a foreign country because of a strong local currency or other factors may strengthen a market that might otherwise be weak and defer any correction to previous rises.
7. The mood of the moment. Though it is hard to measure this quality, a market characterized by great enthusiasm may at least temporarily stay at high levels or go to higher levels than would otherwise be expected.

Factors such as these would be relevant in making strategical decisions within the overall framework of a suitable investment policy for each individual investor or organization.

Reviewing Policy and Strategy

The point was made in earlier chapters that investment portfolios must be subject to constant review. As well as reviewing the particular investment, these reviews should also involve a review of investment policy and strategy.

An investment policy that was appropriate at an earlier time may not be so relevant at present. This could be because the circumstances of the investor have changed in that he or she has retired or is closer to retirement, his/her income situation has changed, his/her commitments in terms of dependants have increased or decreased, or the amount or reliability of income from other sources has changed. There may also be a need for a change because of changing conditions in investment markets.

A good illustration of the latter point is the vast difference between going into equities in the 1950s, when the relative cost was less than 1 (i.e., dividend yield was above interest rate available on fixed interest investments), and going into or staying in the stock market in the early 80s when relevant costs have been above 3.0. Though investment policy and strategy should not be changed lightly, it is probable that one of the major factors in disappointing investment results of recent years has been the tendency of investors to follow the same policy and strategy in the 80s, when equity investments have tended to be very highly priced, as they did in the 50s when they were low priced. If investors do not review their policy and strategy from time to time in the face of changing circumstances, they could suffer the same fate as the manufacturers of horse-drawn carriages about the turn of the century when automobiles were invented, who said that the "horseless carriage" was just a passing fad which was not going to divert them from carrying on their well-established business.

24

Market Cycles, Market Fashions, and the Timing of Investments

Because equity markets, especially stock markets on which there is so much publicity and discussion, tend to be dominated by speculation (with even old established institutions trying to outguess each other in speculating about the future course of the market), there is no way of knowing precisely when a particular market will rise or fall. The old saying that nobody rings a bell at the top or the bottom of the market should not be forgotten. The figures relating to the overall performance of the stock market, the significance of relative costs, and the other matters discussed in Part 4 of the text are all helpful in trying to time moves into and out of equity markets. In this chapter we look at some specific influences on market behavior.

Economic Factors Affecting Investment Markets

The claim made by some people, including those who support the efficient market hypothesis, that stock markets correctly predict economic trends and corporate earnings is far from the truth. It is well to remember the cynic's comment that the stock market is a very good indicator of economic recovery because it has correctly predicted 16 of the last 4 recoveries. The facts are that because of the psychological factors, speculation, changes in perception, moods and fashions, and other factors, the market is by no means solely or even principally affected by economic factors. But obviously a number of economic factors have some effect on the market, and investors need to take these into account.

The major economic factors which affect the investment markets are the following:

1. Economic trends and prospects for the whole economy, both the U.S. economy and the larger world economy of which it forms an important part.
2. Trends in corporate earnings affected partly by economic conditions and partly because of changes in the share of the economic "cake" going to labor and business respectively.
3. Changing conditions and trends in particular industry groups.
4. Trends for particular companies, including not only those due to trends in the industry and in the overall economy, but to factors such as management changes and the development of new products, the switch of resources into more profitable areas, etc.
5. Changes in interest rates or expected changes which may have some effect on the market to the extent to which the theoretical tendency for market prices to vary so that yield would be adjusted in line with changes in interest rates is not offset by any one of a number of other factors.
6. Changes in the law relating to tax shelters, general taxation laws which may make one type of activity more profitable from the "bottom line" point of view, or changes which may affect the major part of the corporate sector such as more favorable investment allowances.

These are among the important factors which investors would need to consider or discuss with their investment adviser in considering the relative attractions of equity markets overall or particular equity investments.

Market-Oriented Factors

An important point made in an earlier chapter which investors must always remember is that a purchase of common stock is not primarily an investment in a company but an investment in a market. What happens in that market, including psychological factors, cycles, and changes in expectation and fashions, may have just as important an effect on an investment as what happens in the company whose stock has been purchased.

Some of the market movement reflects the economic factors discussed above, but often there are what are called market-oriented forces which have a significant effect. Sometimes these may be triggered off by hard economic news. But their influence can be distorted and magnified in some cases and minimized in others by the prevailing mood of the moment. For example, the expected improvement in the U.S. economy which became evident in the second half of 1982 would have been expected to produce some improvement in the market. But it would not have justified the increase of about 50 percent in market prices over a period of six months, especially as stock prices at that time in terms of relative cost were far from the bargain basement.

Moreover, it was not hard economic news which could have justified a rise of over 50 percent in a period of about six to eight months and then almost no rise in the succeeding six months in a period when earlier expectations about improvements in the economy were being seen in the economic recovery, which showed considerable strength in 1983.

Among the market-oriented factors which are very important are the following:

1. *Market cycles.* This is the tendency for markets to move in a wave-like form with prices in bull markets going well above what may be justified on more objective grounds and then in later periods reacting or overreacting to levels well below what may be justified.
2. *The pendulum effect and the hangover analogy.* Just as a long party tonight may mean a worse hangover tomorrow, so an extreme rise in market prices or a prolonged rise may be followed by a more severe and prolonged slump. To put it another way, there is a pendulum effect in which after reaching very high levels based on over-enthusiasm, prices may tend to swing in the opposite direction toward extreme despondency.
3. *Changing fashions in the market* when particular types of investments, particular industries, or particular stocks (the conglomerates of the 1960s, or the gambling stocks of the 70s) may enjoy periods of extreme popularity.
4. *Changing moods.* Depending on whether the prevailing mood is one of optimism or pessimism, perception of information and hard economic news may differ considerably. In bull markets and times of great enthusiasm, markets tend to exaggerate the effect of good news and ignore or substantially disregard bad news. At times of market pessimism when prices have reacted severely to previous excessive enthusiasm, good news may tend to be disregarded and bad news have a greater effect than is warranted on market prices.
5. *Relative cost.* Though markets in times of enthusiasm may tend to ignore high relative costs, there eventually comes a time of reckoning (perhaps because it is not possible to fool all of the people all of the time) so that high relative costs may be a reason for deferring or at least thinking twice about increased investment in an equity market.
6. *Disenchantment.*

Charts of Stock Market Cycles

Below there are simplified charts of U.S. stock market prices as measured by the Dow Jones Industrial Index and the New York Stock Exchange Composite Index (see Charts 24–1A and 24–1B). These charts

Chart 24–1
Simplified Charts of Stock Market Movements Showing Only Major Turning Points*

A. Dow Jones Industrial Index

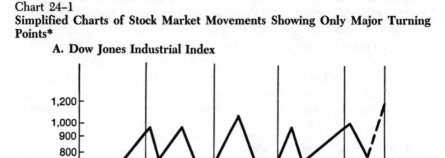

B. New York Stock Exchange Composite Index

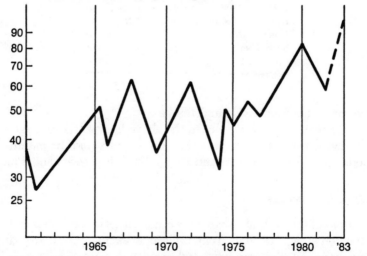

*Dotted lines show movements in present uncompleted cycle.

are simplified in that they show only major turning points. Markets do not, of course, move directly from peak to trough and then back up to the next peak, but go through many sawtooth-like movements with false starts and intermediate swings around the general direction of the market.

Incidentally, a quick comparison of the two indexes will show that the cyclical pattern is fairly similar, but the composite index tended to show a better performance in the 1970s. This could be due to the fact that there was some disenchantment with the performance in terms of earnings and prospects of the limited number of leading stocks in the Dow Jones Index. It could also reflect in part the fact that a wider based index such as the composite index includes a greater representation of "up and coming" stocks in new and growing industries compared with the older established stocks in the Dow Jones Index, which tended to be in mature industries.

Cyclical Peaks and Length of Cycle

On the basis of the Dow Jones Industrial Index, the length of cycles over about the last 20 years can be seen from the figures below (measured from peak to peak):

Period	Index	Period from Previous Peak
December 1961	735	—
February 1966	995	4 yrs. 2 mos.
December 1968	985	2 yrs. 10 mos.
January 1973	1,052	4 yrs. 1 mos.
September 1976	1,015	3 yrs. 8 mos.
April 1981	1,024	4 yrs. 7 mos.

Average Length of Cycle and Range

For the five completed cycles in the above figures, the average period of the cycle from peak to peak was three years and 10 months. The periods range from two years and 10 months to four years and 7 months.

Significance of Declines

The extent of the cyclical movements can perhaps be best seen by looking at the percentage decline from cyclical peak to cyclical trough. The figures based on the Dow Jones Industrial Index are as follows:

Period from Peak to Trough	Percentage Decline
December 1961 to June 1962	21.7
February 1966 to October 1966	25.3
December 1968 to May 1970	35.9
January 1973 to December 1974	45.2
September 1976 to February 1978	26.8
April 1981 to August 1982	24.2

Average Decline and Range

On the six figures included above, the average decline from peak to trough was 29.8 percent. The range was from 21.7 to 45.2 percent. The largest decline of 45.2 percent between January 1973 and December 1974 was in the period when the first oil crisis had serious effects on business confidence as well as triggering off inflationary pressures which were problems for many companies. That was also the period when interest rates rose sharply in most countries to levels well above the highest that had been experienced in the previous few decades.

Long-Term Trend in the Market

If an investor happened to go into the market at the low point in June 1962 and sell out at the low point in August 1982 and his/her portfolio was the same as that represented by the Dow Jones Index, he or she would have seen an increase of about 45 percent (June 1962 index of 536 and August 1982 index of 776). Over the period of just over 20 years, this would have represented a growth rate of 1.85 percent per annum compound. If we look at the high points and consider an investor who invested in December 1961 and sold at the peak of 1981, that investor would have enjoyed an increase of 39 percent. Over the 19.3-year period this is equivalent to a growth rate of 1.72 percent per annum compound. Approximately similar results would have been achieved over that period by a person who bought at about the midpoint of the cycle and sold at a similar point. Obviously, the person who bought at the low point in June 1962 and sold at any of the succeeding high points would have done considerably better. On the other hand, the person who bought at a high point in the cycle and sold, or perhaps had to sell, at a low point in the cycle may have suffered a significant loss.

The Combined Problems of Cyclical Movements and Lower Growth

The effect of cycles on investment results has been a more significant problem in the last 10 to 20 years than in earlier years. The reason is that in earlier years the fairly rapid upward trend of share prices would offset in a few years any adverse cyclical movements for the person who was unfortunate enough to invest at the peak of a cycle. For example, in the 1950s and early 60s when stock prices were rising in an upward trend rate of about 6 to 7 percent per annum, a decline of 20 percent or so suffered by the person who bought at the peak would be substantially offset in a few years by the rapidly rising market tide, so to speak. In more recent years, when the tide has been flowing less strongly, cyclical slumps can be more serious.

Intelligent Market Study Preferable to Mechanical Charting

One approach to investing attempts to predict future market movements, either for the whole market such as the stock market, for particular stocks, or for industry groups, by what is called charting. This is based on the belief that when market prices are plotted on a chart, patterns can be detected in which future market movements can be predicted. Some people who are convinced that prediction of future price movements and hence investment success can be determined simply from studying charts, would say that they can make their predictions without knowing anything about the economic conditions, earnings, industry prospects, or any other fundamental factors relating to a particular investment.

That claim and many of the other claims made by chartists are not soundly based. The fact that sometimes in the past a particular pattern on a chart has been followed by a particular price movement does not necessarily mean that similar movement following that sort of pattern is inevitable or even probable in the future. Obviously, all sorts of other factors such as changes in interest rates, economic conditions, and other factors discussed in this chapter could have a bearing.

Even though following what might be called the mechanistic approach to trying to apply the practices of charting is not a logical approach to investing, experience suggests that some of the points made by chartists have some validity. In particular, the following points are worth considering in making decisions about timing of investments:

1. The concept of support of, and resistance to, price movements.
2. The significance of a break in an upward trend which had been established for some time.
3. The recognition of the importance of volume, especially in relation to potential market rises.

The chartist's idea of support is that there may be certain price levels at which significant buying pressure could provide substantial support for a stock and hence halt and possibly reverse any downward trend in prices. The idea of resistance is that there are certain levels where potential selling presure could halt and perhaps reverse any rising trend in prices.

As for the areas in which support or resistance is likely to occur, one possibility is areas in which there has been significant trading in the past. A glance at the chart may show that in the past, prices stayed around a certain level for a significant time. If the chart also contains details of volumes of trading which indicate that volumes were relatively heavy at that time, that could be a further indication of possible support or resistance around that level. Round figure price levels such as $10, $20, $50, or $100 are also potential areas of support and resistance. The reason is that a lot of people decide that they will buy if the price reduces to one of these levels or sell if it increases to another round figure level. Incidentally, one practical aspect that arises out of this is that it is often unwise to decide that you will sell a stock when it reaches $30, $50, or whatever. It is far better to make a selling decision when your consideration of both market study and other factors such as relative cost, prospects for the company, interest rate trends, and other matters discussed in this chapter indicate that at least some selling action may be appropriate.

Chartists say that if prices have been trading for a reasonable period, such as a year or 18 months, above a certain trend line (an upward trend line is the line joining the low points of the intermediate downswings on a semilogarithmic chart where a straight line indicates a constant rate of change in price and not a constant amount of change), then this is a good reason for selling the stock. While it is not an infallible sign, such a break of trend often is an indicator of change of market sentiments as it shows that, for whatever reason, there has not been in the present instance sufficient buying interest to lift prices up above the trend line as has occurred in the past.

The third aspect of charting practices which can be useful is the recognition of volume, especially in relation to rises in price. There is an old saying with a good deal of merit that stocks can fall under their own weight, but they need volume to push them up. It is reasonable to assume that price rises accompanied by significant and increasing volume may be more significant in terms of the strength of the market and its possible future price movements in the short term than a price rise on insignificant or declining volume.

Perhaps the most practical approach to this question of timing is to use the three practices above which are applied by chartists in what could be called market study. This involves looking at a chart of prices for a particular market or particular stock to at least get some idea of how prices have been moving. If you see that in the recent past prices have been going up very rapidly (an almost vertical line on the chart), it is probable that that rate of rise will not be maintained indefinitely. As steep rises of that type often occur in the latter stages of a bull market, it may be a warning that the cyclical dowturn could be imminent.

Rapidly Rising Trends Unlikely to Be Maintained

Another significant aspect of market study that is worth remembering is that rapidly rising price trends are less likely to be maintained than trends rising at a more gradual rate. Perhaps this point could be visualized by making a paraphrase of the statement referred to earlier in the text, attributed to Abraham Lincoln, that you can fool all of the people some of the time or some of the people all of the time, but you cannot fool all of the people all of the time. Applied to trends in relation to prices, this would be paraphrased roughly by saying that you can have gradual rising trends maintained for a long time, or sharply rising trends maintained for a short time, but you cannot have sharply rising trends maintained for a long time.

This can be confirmed by having a look at charts of almost any market, whether stock markets, real estate markets, commodities, or whatever. Almost without exception, prices that rise in a relatively gradual manner tend to maintain that rise for a much longer period than those where the rise is sharp.

Another important point to remember is that few investments have been able to maintain in the long term (10 to 20 years or more) a rate of increase in value much above the 10 to 15 percent per annum range.

Estimating a Normal Trading Range for a Market

Whenever markets suffer a severe fall, all sorts of reasons are advanced for it. Generally, the main reason, the fact that prices had reached far too high a level, is seldom discussed. The reasons that are advanced as the cause of the decline are more likely to be the trigger actions which precipitated the inevitable reaction to the past excesses. So it may be helpful to try to estimate the normal trading range for a market, allowing for cyclical movements above and below a line that may represent an estimate of the general direction of the market. If this is done, price moves well above that range could be considered as a boom area to be followed by the inevitable bust. This exercise is likely to act as a warning against enthusiastic movement into markets that have gone well into the boom area from which a decline is not so much a matter of "if" as of "when."

Remember that this is not an attempt to make a precise prediction of future market trends, but rather it is an attempt to indicate the range within which normal trading may be expected to take place. It is not intended as a precise forecasting tool, but simply as a means of sounding some sort of warning bell when prices move into areas which are unlikely to be maintained.

Below there is a chart showing estimated normal price range for common stocks based on the New York Stock Exchange Composite Index (see Chart 24-2). This exercise was done in June 1983. You will see that it indicated that from the end of 1982, prices have been moving up into what seemed to be a boom area similar to booms in the early 80s and the mid-70s from which the inevitable sharp reaction later took place.

The exercise of estimating normal price range involves, first, calculation of a base line for the range. This line is in market study terms the upward trend line (joining low points) above which all trading has taken place for a medium-term period (usually several years). A medium term is used to eliminate the distorting effect of sharp short-term variations. By joining the low points and extending the line, we arrive at the base for the normal trading range.

The extension of that upward trend line into future time periods gives us the base of the estimated normal trading range. The upper limit is a line drawn parallel to the base line. Remember that by using semi-logarithmic (or ratio) chart paper, straight lines mean a constant rate of change (e.g., 10 percent per annum compound from 100 to 110 in one year, 121 in two years, 133 in three years).

In most markets the normal range (excluding the periodical price zoom up to a dizzy height and the later correction) is about 25 to 30 percent. So the top boundary of the estimated normal range is arrived at by some

Chart 24-2

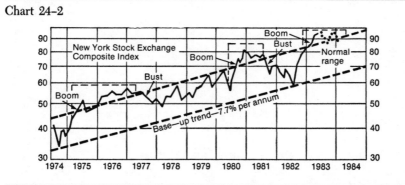

experimenting to find a line that is the upper limit of trading for most of the time and is about 25 to 30 percent above the base line. The aim is not to find a line with great precision, but to make a reasonable estimate of the line which seems to be top of the range for most of the time except for the booms and corrections.

Normal Trading Range for the Stock Market

Chart 24–2 shows the estimated normal trading range for the U.S. stock market based on the New York Stock Exchange Composite Index. It was prepared in May 1983 and has been brought up to the time of writing—the dotted line showing the movements since it was first prepared.

It remains to be seen whether the future movements of the market in the later months of 1983 and beyond will be a continuation of the down trend back into the normal range. Though it is not a magic answer to all timing problems, it certainly was a useful reminder in mid-1983 that the market had moved into a dangerously high area—at a time when many comments suggested that further sustained gain was absolutely assured.

25

Investing in Bonds and Other Low Risk Areas

Some investors say that bonds and other fixed interest investments are not for real investors but are suitable only for financial pikers. Some of those who believe that there can be a place for at least part of the total portfolio being in fixed interest investments reply that it may be better to be a solvent financial piker than a bankrupt or financially embarrassed adventurer in more exciting investments. Some investors who entered into fixed interest investments early in 1980, resisting the temptation to go into gold, which was then described as the ultimate hedge against inflation that would protect the real value of their investments, have avoided the decline of over 50 percent in the price of gold since that time. (They have also received significant income which investors in gold sacrificed because of their faith in the hard currency that some of them would now be inclined to rename as the hard luck currency.)

A Caution about Risk

In describing bonds and other fixed interest investments as being in the low risk area, it is necessary to remember the point made earlier. That point was that in assigning various risk categories to investments, it was on the basis that normal precautions have been taken in the selection of investments and are spread over different investments. The person who unwisely put a large amount of his or her money in bonds of an unsound company or in a mortgage loan on an overvalued property to a financially weak borrower would not be enjoying the benefits of a low risk investment.

There is also the point that even in investments that are safe from the viewpoint of receipt of interest and repayment of capital on maturity, there is the risk associated with interest rate changes. Especially on medium- to long-term fixed interest investments, a subsequent increase in the general level of interest rates can cause a decline in capital value (a risk that can be minimized by concentrating investments in the short- to medium-term period to maturity).

Subject to those comments, this area is a relatively low risk area primarily because there is contractual obligation for payment of interest and repayment of capital. Investors also may enjoy safety afforded by security over investments or by a buffer comprised of the claims of stockholders or junior securities which rank behind them.

Range of Investments

In the low risk area of fixed interest investments, there is a fairly wide range. It includes banks which are members of the Federal Deposit Insurance Corporation, which insures deposits in member banks up to $100,000 for each depositor; federally chartered savings and loan organizations with similar protection; federal, state, and local government securities; bonds of corporations; mortgages; and participation in these investments through bond mutual funds and pass through mortgage certificates.

Private loans to individuals or businesses would also be in the low risk category if the earning capacity and cash flow of the borrower are more than adequate to meet interest and capital repayment commitments.

Plus and Minus Factors

One of the main plus factors for this type of investment is the greatest safety and relatively low risk compared to other investments (subject to the comments earlier in the chapter in relation to the caution on risk). Another is the fact that the income return is known in advance and is fixed in contrast to equity investments, where it may vary considerably and the income could be nil in the event of poor business conditions or tight liquidity. In direct business investments the result could be a loss. Repayment of capital at a fixed future date is another advantage which helps future financial planning.

As for the minus factors, perhaps the main disadvantage is that the fixed interest investor does not normally "get a slice of the action." In a highly successful company in which equity investors may enjoy increasing income and substantial capital gain, the fixed interest investor receives simply the agreed income and the repayment of his or her capital on maturity (except for some special arrangements with some fixed interest investments which incorporate some of the features of equities).

For investors in the medium to high income tax brackets, the tax burden on the income may make these investments less attractive than others providing a lower income return but substantial capital gain on which the tax burden is less. Some investors would also consider it a disadvantage that the fixed interest investor does not have the sense of participating in the earnings and growth of a listed company and the excitement that goes with watching developments, perhaps switching from one stock to another in a more active management of an equity portfolio. (This excitement may, of course, be a good deal less appealing to the equity investor when the market tide has turned and prices decline seriously.)

Use of These Investments by Various Investors

The extent to which fixed interest investments should be used by individual investors depends on their particular situation—the circumstances that were discussed in Chapter 23 dealing with investment policy and strategy, Chapter 13 dealing with risk category for various investors, and Chapter 14 dealing with the risk categories for various investments. Briefly, for the person who has limited income from other sources, limited capital, is getting on in years, and has little or no future working life to rebuild any capital loss out of subsequent earnings, the low risk fixed interest investments may necessarily have to make up all or the major part of his or her portfolio.

At the other extreme, the investor with relatively large capital and adequate, assured income from some other sources who is fairly young, with many years of future working life may wish to limit his or her commitment to fixed interest investments to a small part of the total. For such a person, the wise idea may be to have at all times a small portion of the total investment in this area—perhaps 20 percent or so—as a sheet anchor to provide some protection against sudden severe declines in equity markets. That portion could be increased temporarily at times when equity markets look vulnerable to decline to provide a temporary haven for funds that would otherwise be in the equity market. Such a switch of funds could protect capital against the results of a severe decline and ensure that funds are available for switching back into equities at more realistic prices in the future.

The medium risk investor, who represents a large percentage of the total number of investors in between the two extreme categories described above, could see wisdom in having a minimum percentage of about 30 to 40 percent in fixed interest investments (a larger sheet anchor than for the larger investor better able to face risks). Again, this investor could increase that percentage to 60 to 80 percent at times when equity markets are very vulnerable to imminent decline.

Period to Maturity

In considering the period to maturity of fixed interest investments, one point to consider is that the risk of decline in capital value due to subsequent changes in interest rate levels is greater on longer dated maturities. The investor who wishes to minimize that risk can do so by limiting his or her investments to medium-term periods of up to five years. Even a significant rise in interest rate levels in the economy a year or so later will have a relatively small effect because there are only 3 or 4 years to maturity compared with the effect on investments with 10 to 15 years or more to maturity. Another factor to be considered is the cash needs of the investor for any major purposes such as the purchase of a home, establishment of a business, prolonged foreign trips, or other purposes.

It is also a good plan to spread investments over different maturities. This means that funds are available at different times, which facilitates the making of reinvestment decisions in the light of up-to-date information on interest rate trends, cash needs, and other factors. For bonds which are listed, it may be argued that the maturity does not matter all that much because they can be sold on the market. This is true, but market sales are subject to risk of the effect of changes in interest rates. Hence, there is some merit in having a portfolio which enables access to funds at various dates in the future, arises on maturity, and is not dependent on market values.

Principles to Be Applied in Selecting, Reviewing, and Controlling Investments

In discussing the selection of fixed interest investments with clients, I often refer to a sign, for the benefit of staff, which I saw in a barracks store in World War II. It said, "Put your trust in God and get a signature from everybody else." Applied to the selection of fixed interest investments, this could be adapted to put your trust in an objective analysis and don't rely unduly on well-known names. For investments which are not guaranteed or assured, such as bank and savings and loan deposits covered by Federal Deposit Insurance Corporation, it is necessary to consider the factors which provide protection for the fixed interest investor.

One of these is the margin comprised of the buffer of stockholders' funds and the funds of junior securities which rank behind the investor. If that figure is expressed as a percentage of total assets, it shows what proportion of total assets could be lost through trading losses or in liquidation before the fixed interest investors' capital is put in jeopardy. Another point is to consider any minimum margin of safety which arises as the result of any provisions in deeds which require the borrowing company to maintain certain relationships between liabilities and assets. Trends in earnings and in cash flow are also relevant.

After looking at those positive factors, it is then important to look at any specific areas of risk. This could include such questions as heavy investment in speculative property development, which could cause problems in the event of tight money conditions or high interest rates making it difficult to refinance maturing loans. Undue concentration of lending by a financial institution to one or a few clients, especially those associated with the company, may also be another danger sign. So too would be any above normal risks in the type of business in which the borrower operates. If any of those risk factors are significant, it may be wise to look elsewhere, even if the positive factors discussed above look fairly healthy. This is a case where it is wise to apply the principle "if in doubt—stay out."

If long-term investment is being considered, it may be wise to concentrate a larger proportion of funds in government type securities rather than commercial securities. The reason is that the longer the period, the greater the chance that a company which appears to be in a healthy position now may go through an adverse change of conditions.

As for reviewing and controlling investments, it is not so vital a function in fixed interest investments as in equities, where there are so many other variables to be considered. But it does not mean that fixed interest investments should be completely forgotten about. Close attention to trends in interest rates, including consideration of opinions on this matter from specialists in the area, may help in deciding on questions such as the period for which maturing investments should be reinvested and the wisdom or otherwise of taking a profit on any fixed interest investments that have risen in value because of a subsequent change in interest rates, or holding in anticipation of further benefit.

Investment through Bond Funds

For the investor who does not want to be involved in selecting and managing his or her own fixed interest investments directly, there are various types of bond funds now available. These are mutual funds invested in bonds so that an individual investor can obtain the benefit of a wider spread than he or she would be able to obtain directly and the benefit of investment expertise in selecting and managing these investments. He or she would have to weigh those benefits against the costs involved in the management fees and/or initial service charges applicable to that investment.

26

Investing in the Stock Market

The comments in this and the next chapter should not be considered in isolation. All of the information in earlier chapters is relevant. In particular, the first two chapters dealing with the need to get back to the three Rs of investing, financial fables, fallacies, and folklore are essential preliminary considerations. So are Chapters 7 and 8 dealing with possible sources of capital gain and loss, the chapters in Part 3 dealing with risk and investments, and Chapters 19 to 22 inclusive dealing with the relative cost of U.S. stocks, the importance of relative costs on stock investing, the process of calculating capital gain targets, and the chance of achieving and seeing relative cost figures in correct perspective.

Plus and Minus Factors

One of the main plus factors for common stock investment is that it enables investors to "get a slice of the action." (The French word for stock or equity is indeed *action*.) Investors in common stocks feel a sense of participation in the fortunes of the companies in which they have invested and derive, in many cases, a good deal of interest from watching the progress of that company, studying market trends and the large amount of information that is available. The fact that so much information is available is an advantage for this type of investment compared to others (though there is the need to allow for the information and accounting risk discussed in earlier chapters). Another significant advanage of this type of investment is that it is a very liquid investment. An investor needing cash can sell stocks in a short time, except for stocks which may be listed only on the small regional exchanges or the less active section of the over-the-counter market.

Arising out of that liquidity situation is also the fact that stock investments are easily divisible. Except for the very small investor who may face the additional cost of odd lot dealings, it is possible to "fine tune" the overall portfolio or the holdings of particular stock by selling 5 percent, 10 percent, 12 percent, or whatever of a particular holding. This is a facility generally not available in other investments such as real estate, except for very large investors who may sell one of a large number of holdings.

Some investors see as a particular advantage of the stock market that it offers such a wide range of investments, including some which are relatively stable and others which are highly volatile and speculative, so that it caters to the needs of a wide range of investors with different viewpoints.

On the minus side, the reverse side of the coin to the liquidity and readily available information is that stock markets tend to be more volatile. This volatile movement tends to offset some of the advantages of liquidity in that some would say liquidity doesn't mean much if converting an investment into cash at a particular time involves a significant loss because the market is going through the lower part of its cyclical movement.

In recent years, for reasons which have been outlined earlier in the book, increasing speculation, including speculation by large institutions trying to outguess each other about the future course of the market, has tended to make it more volatile and has increased the risk. For this reason, the stock market has to be regarded as a medium to high risk investment. It is necessary to remember the point made elsewhere in the text that so-called first class investments and blue chip stocks are in fact medium to high risk investments because of this volatile market movement.

Scope for Various Types of Investors

For the investor with limited funds available and little or no income from other sources, or the investor who is getting on in years with little or no future working life to rebuild capital after any adverse market experiences, it may be necessary to stay out of the stock market or to limit one's commitment to a small percentage of perhaps 5 to 10 percent of one's total portfolio. At the other end of the scale, the investor who can afford high to very high risks, such as the person with adequate capital, adequate and assured income from other sources, and many years of future working life, the commitment of a large portion of one's total portfolio to common stocks would be practicable. This is not to say that such an investor should always aim to have all or the major part of his or her funds in the stock market. You will recall from the previous chapter that such a person could see merit in having a portion of his or her investments, say 20 percent, in the fixed interest area as a sort of sheet anchor for protection from sudden serious market declines. There would also be a case for him or her to consider other types of equity investments such as real estate and possibly some commitment to the higher risk investments such as gold, silver, commodities, and futures trading discussed in later chapters.

Because markets fluctuate considerably, the relatively high risk investor could also see merit in reducing his or her investment in equities when they seem to be vulnerable to imminent cyclical decline. Funds could at that stage be switched out of equities to temporarily increase the investor's fixed interest holdings with the idea of switching them back into the stock market after the slump, when common stocks are available at more realistic prices.

In the intermediate category, the medium risk person may see merit in having up to 60 percent in this market (or a smaller proportion if he or she has other investments in medium or high risk areas) when market conditions seem favorable and a smaller percentage of 20 to 30 percent when markets appear vulnerable to cyclical decline.

Factors Affecting the Overall Market

Essentially, the result of investment in the stock market depends on two components—the course of the stock market overall and the extent to which a particular stock or stocks perform relative to the rest of the market. So we first look at a summary of the major factors which can affect the market overall.

Economic Factors

1. Trends in economic growth due to the effect of factors such as population growth, development of new technology, and the trend toward more or less utilization of the whole resources of the economy.
2. The effect of trends in world trade on the local economy.
3. Government policies in matters such as direct taxation and indirect taxation which can change spending patterns.
4. Trends in interest rates.

Corporate Sector of the Economy

1. The cost of capital comprised of both interest rates and the cost of equity capital, reflecting the situation of the stock market.
2. Trends in the share of gross domestic product accruing to the

business sector, reflecting such factors as the bargaining position of business relative to labor.
3. Utilization of industrial capacity.
4. The financial structure of the corporate sector overall in terms of its ability to raise further funds from retained earnings or capital issues.
5. Costs and administrative burdens of environmental protection, which may benefit society at the expense of the corporate sector.

Market-Oriented Factors

1. Interest rate effects on the market, reflecting changing attraction of other investments and a trend toward equity market yields to adjust in line with interest rate trends.
2. Currency changes (i.e., of the local currency relative to major foreign currencies) which could affect the attraction of the local stock market to foreign investors.
3. Market cycles—or more particularly, the extent to which cycles are accentuated by market factors beyond the effect which would be expected from basic economic forces.
4. The mood of the moment, the extent to which the stock market is "the flavor of the month" for investors, or the effect of disenchantment following earlier excessive rises.
5. The selling of stock market investments, including mutual funds, could at times push markets up higher than may be warranted and later cause reactions in the other direction.

The factors listed above are those which an investor needs to recognize and consider in relation to the overall stock market before proceeding to look at the factors which affect individual stocks.

Factors Affecting Particular Stocks

In general, most stocks tend to be affected by the same sort of influences. At times when markets are very low, such as 1974, nearly all stocks are affected; at times when markets rise substantially, as in 1982–83, most stocks tend to enjoy that benefit. There are differences in the time at which rises and declines commence and in the extent of those movements, but most stocks tend to go with the tide.

Having decided that a certain amount of capital is to be invested in the stock market, the next step is to be aware of those factors which could affect individual stocks to make their performance better or worse than that of the market overall. These factors are summarized briefly below.

1. *Industry prospects.* Because stocks in which scope for profitable growth is greater, for example, in new innovative industries in contrast with some of the older, more mature industries, could be expected to do better (except to the extent to which that benefit has already been anticipated or overanticipated—see comments below).

2. *Relative earnings.* If a stock is likely to produce growth and earnings considerably better than the average for stocks generally, it would be expected to increase in value at a faster rate than the general market.

3. *Changes in market rating.* Market rating is the price of the stock as measured by the dividend yield or the price earnings multiple relative to the overall market average. If the market becomes enchanted with the performance or prospects of a particular stock or group of stocks, then in addition to the market price rising to reflect the actual or expected better earnings performance, there may be an additional benefit through the stock being given a higher market rating—for example, an increase in the price earnings multiple from 10 to 15. Conversely, if a stock has already had its market rating increased significantly, perhaps doubled in the last year or two, there could be less scope for further improvement in market value from that particular source. (Indeed, if there has been a rapid increase in market rating leading to some overanticipation, there could be a decline in market rating which could offset some of the improvement in price due to the earnings performance.)

4. *Mood of the moment and momentum.* A stock or a group of stocks at the top of the Wall Street hit parade in a concentrated burst of short-term enthusiasm could do better than would otherwise be expected, but stocks which have fallen from grace may lag behind.

5. *Selling enthusiasm.* If a particular stock or funds invested in particular stocks or industries are being very actively promoted, this could push prices up faster than expected.

Indicators Favorable to the Stock Market

As timing is so important in stock market investments, a decision to move substantially into the market or to stay substantially in it (subject to policy decisions discussed earlier) could be made more confidently when various indicators point to that being a favorable time. Among the most important indicators are the following:

1. *The relative cost.* For reasons discussed at length in Part 4, a high relative cost increases the target figure for required capital gain and tends to lessen the chance of achieving the gain. If past experience is any guide, a relative cost in the range of 1.2 to 2.0 may be consid-

ered favorable and a figure in the range of 2.5 and above unfavorable.

2. *Expectations.* As this reflects relative cost, the same principle applies.

3. *Cyclical position.* If a chart shows that the market after a slump shows signs of recovering, that could be favorable, especially if it is in the lower phase of its normal trading range discussed in an earlier chapter.

4. *Momentum.* If the market tends to indicate considerable buying strength with no sign of a likely sell signal from the Coppock Indicator of possible turning points based on a smoothed moving average of market movements compared with 12 months previously, the market would be more attractive.

5. *Success of investment selling.* There is ample evidence that selling of investment in common stocks, especially through mutual funds invested in that market producing results, then that would be a favorable indicator.

6. Favorable trends in the factors relating to the economy and the corporate sector discussed earlier in the chapter.

Indicators Unfavorable to the Stock Market

In general, indicators opposite to those set out above would be unfavorable toward the stock market. They would tend to indicate that it is not the time for increased investment and could indeed be the time for reducing investment in that market.

The Problem of Mixed Indicators

If there was a situation where all the indicators were favorable or unfavorable, decisions would be fairly simple. However, this situation seldom arises, and the investor is generally faced with a situation where some indicators are favorable and some are unfavorable. This means that the investor must make a judgment as to what is the predominant tendency. This is not simply a matter of counting up the favorable and unfavorable factors, but involves trying to assess the overall picture.

As a general rule, there is probably a case for applying more weight to the market-oriented factors. The reason is that even if logic in terms of economic trends, trends in the corporate sector, and other factors indicated that the market was somewhat overpriced, there might still be opportunities in it if market factors were very favorable. However, it is well to have regard to factors such as relative costs on the basis that, in the short term, realities may take second place to market sentiment or severe despondency, but in the medium to longer term, realities tend to emerge.

Short-Term Trading

The comments in this chapter and to a considerable extent throughout the book are designed primarily for the medium- to long-term investor rather than the short-term trader. A few brief comments here may be of interest to those considering trading.

Trading in stocks is not the short-term path to riches which a number of people, including quite a few authors, have made it out to be. There are several qualities which an investor needs in order to undertake any significant amount of short-term trading. One is to have sufficient capital to be able to devote a part to this relatively high risk operation without placing his or her basic capital or next week's housekeeping money in jeopardy. Another is to ensure that he or she has the time to watch the market closely, not only by the day but by the hour—a somewhat difficult problem for the busy executive, professional person, or homemaker. To the old saying (modified slightly to eliminate sexist phrases) that time and tide wait for no person could be added, neither does the stock market. If the market is inclined to go into a slump, the fact that you are away on vacation, extremely busy at the office, or facing a family crisis at home will not persuade it to defer its decline until you are better able to cope with it.

The other quality which the trader needs is the right temperament— the temperament to make decisions fairly quickly, to make unpleasant decisions to cut losses when markets have not cooperated with his or her predictions, and the ability to apply as logical an approach as possible in a fairly tumultuous arena.

Preferred Stock

Holders of preferred stock are entitled to be paid a certain rate of dividend before any dividend can be paid to common stock holders. Though this makes preferred stock less risky than common stock, it does not afford as much safety as fixed interest investments. There is no contractual obligation to pay a dividend each year or to repay the amount invested—simply a requirement that the preferred dividend must be paid before any dividend can be paid on common stock. No dividend would be paid if the company made a loss, or if it made a profit but a tight cash position or other circumstances led to a decision not to pay any dividends. There is a wide range of different conditions applying to particular issues of preferred stock, so investors need to check carefully on the conditions of any issue in which they may be interested.

Convertible Notes

This type of investment is initially in the nature of a fixed interest investment with a legal obligation to pay interest. But instead of the amount invested being repaid as in the case of regular fixed interest investments, on a prescribed date the notes are converted into shares at a conversion basis included in the original terms of issue. Some investors regard them as a form of deferred equity issue with lower downside risk in the period prior to conversion, as the interest return tends to provide a figure below which prices are unlikely to fall regardless of the movement in the common stock of the relevant company.

27

Investing in the Stock Market (continued)

Turning from consideration of the stock market overall, with a brief comment on short-term trading which was covered in the last chapter, we now turn to considerations related to particular stocks and the specifics of stock market investing.

Indicators Favorable to Particular Stocks

On the principle that it is easy to get ahead when the tide is with you, it is generally better to consider investment in particular stocks when the overall stock market position is favorable as discussed in the previous chapter. But there could be occasions when exceptionally good prospects for a particular stock may enable it to resist the overall market tide at least for a period. In looking at indicators that would be favorable to a particular stock, the following would be among the most important.

1. A reasonable relative cost for the stock so that the required capital gain is not unduly high and the prospects of achieving it would thus be greater.
2. A reasonable market rating providing scope for an increase in capital value in addition to any reflecting either overall market movements or the earnings performance of the stock (see comments in the previous chapter on factors affecting a particular stock).
3. Good earnings prospects relative to expected market average.
4. A favorable market study situation with the chart showing that the downtrend has been broken and the stock shows signs of moving upward.
5. Some support areas of possible buying pressure nearby and no significant resistance levels of serious potential selling pressure close to present price levels.

6. Relatively good industry prospects and popularity in the market. Heavy investment selling—the stock or the industry is one which has been the subject of extensive selling by mutual fund and possibly other investment people, or frequent favorable references in the financial press.

Indicators Unfavorable to a Particular Stock and the Problems of Mixed Indicators

Indicators that would be unfavorable to a particular stock would in general be the reverse of those which are mentioned above. As with indicators for the overall market, investors more frequently face the situation of some favorable and some unfavorable factors.

As indicated in the comments in the previous chapter on indicators for the overall market, an intelligent judgment must then be made. In general, it would be wiser to concentrate on the market-oriented effects such as market rating or market study position for the reasons outlined in Chapter 26.

The Crucial Importance of Price

It is important to remember that although you may speak of investing in XYZ stock, you are really investing in a market. What happens in the market in terms of changes in market sentiments, cycles, fashions, mood of the moment, and other factors may be more significant to your success or failure than what happens in the company itself.

For this reason, it is extremely important to remember that prices are crucial. It may often be wiser to buy a stock with an ordinary or average record and prospects that is realistially priced than a prestigious stock, or a stock with excellent earnings record and prospects, which has been pushed up to a very high level in the market.

The Basic Process of Selecting Stocks

The process of selecting stocks commences with the question of whether some funds should be committed to the stock market and, if so, what portion of the total. The next step is to consider whether the present seems an appropriate time for making an investment, increasing an investment, or in the case of a review of an investment, maintaining an investment in the stock market. The next step is then to consider the factors that have been discussed in this and the previous chapter in trying to arrive at the best combination of reward and risk. As far as possible, you should try to see that there appears to be scope for further increase in value of the stock and that the downside risk is not excessive.

Although nobody rings a bell at the top of the market, the more a stock has risen, the closer it must be drawing to its ultimate peak, wherever that may turn out to be. Moreover, the further it has risen, the greater is the potential for decline when the market tide turns.

Amount for Investment in Each Stock

In deciding how much to invest in each stock, the goal should be to find the happy medium between two extremes. One extreme is an unbalanced portfolio with large amounts in one or a few stocks. The other extreme is a very widely diversified portfolio with the funds spread over a great number of stocks. The first alternative is undesirable because it means that the risk is greater. Any serious reverse for one or two stocks may have a major effect on the whole portfolio. The other extreme, though relatively safe, is troublesome and costly because it means the portfolio is fragmented rather than consolidated.

The ideal is to consolidate the portfolio into a number of stocks which is large enough to give a reasonable spread and hence reduce the risk, but small enough to watch them closely in the process of controlling and managing your portfolio. For most individual investors, this would be somewhere between 6 and 15 stocks.

Managing, Review, and Judicious Selling

Unless you decide to take the path of investing through mutual funds, which is discussed in a later chapter, it is most important that once you go into the stock market you realize that this is an investment which has to be managed and reviewed. The first step is to keep your records up-to-date by at least listing the portfolio either monthly or weekly. With the stocks valued at current prices you can see how they are moving.

At regular intervals, perhaps every three or six months, you need to do an overall review of your portfolio and indeed of your general investment strategy which should be far more comprehensive than the "quick glance" at the portfolio at weekly or monthly intervals. For this purpose, it is essential to stress the point made previously that you must consider each of your investments in relation to its current market value and not to the cost price which you may have paid some time in the past.

Remember the importance of the portfolio effect. If you have one stock or one industry group which is a relatively high proportion of your overall portfolio, then it needs to be given particular attention. The reason is that a decline in that stock or that group of stocks would have a greater effect than a similar decline in other stocks which do not represent such a significant part of the total.

As selling is such an integral part of successful portfolio management, you have to overcome the psychological difficulty which many people face in making selling decisions. It is well to remember the old definition, "An executive is a person who makes quick decisions and is right some of the time." Though you should make your decisions as carefully as possible, you have to accept the fact that some of your decisions will be wrong. For that reason you should not defer selling action simply because of the nagging doubt that perhaps prices may rise later if you sell. You can also use the step system (sell immediately part of the total planned sales, then watch the market closely for the timing of further sales).

You should be prepared to sell and take a profit where an assessment of the situation indicates that scope for further profit could be limited and downside risk may be increasing. You should also be prepared to sell to cut a loss where the market has not cooperated with your predictions if an objective assessment suggests that there is a greater probability of the stock going downward or at best sideways rather than moving up in the near future.

You should be prepared to switch stocks, moving out of one and into another if you think that the second stock offers better prospects. Obviously, because there are some costs involved, both the transaction cost and the time involved in making these decisions, the switch decisions should not be made lightly. On the other hand, you want to avoid falling into the trap of the jellyfish philosophy of simply drifting up and down with the market tide.

The Use of Personal Computers

Many investors today are using their personal computers to help them in their investment management. Computers can help in keeping records of the portfolio up-to-date—especially where you can use a modem to get automatic input of prices for your stocks from a central service. One such system which some investors have found useful is the *Portfolio Evaluation and Reporting System* (PEAR) available from Pear Systems, Stamford, Connecticut, which can be used on popular brands of computers such as the IBM and Apple II.

Other programs are available which can be used to help in switching from stocks when justified by the computer tracking the number of stocks in addition to those in your portfolio. This enables you to switch out of a stock which is not performing up to expectations into one which may have better prospects.

The textbook *The Investor's Computer Handbook* by Rod E. Packer, published by Hayden Book Company of Rochelle Park, New Jersey, has a good deal of useful information on this subject.

Buying Stocks for Recovery

Over the years some investors have done well by selling at a high price some stocks which they had bought earlier at a lower price prior to the market for that stock recovering from earlier declines due to company problems. In a way this is an application of the traditional advice to "buy in gloom, sell in boom."

If you are considering this approach, do not make the mistake of thinking that every stock which has gone through difficulties and shown some signs of recovery is going to provide a bonanza. Sometimes the market has a long memory, and it may be a considerable time before a stock which has fallen from grace is restored to anything like its earlier market rating. For this reason, it is often wise to satisfy yourself that not only the fortunes of the company have improved but the market rating of the company is also in the process of being restored.

Takeovers

From time to time investors have done well by buying stocks not long before a successful takeover bid has been made at a higher price. Theoretically, all you have to do is select a stock with assets well above its present market value, which is not making full use of those assets and which could be attractive to a larger company or a more efficient company that may be able to use them more effectively.

One of the problems is that a stock which may be a takeover prospect may not produce good profits if so many people think it is a takeover prospect that they bid its price up to a level which is not far below what would be offered by an acquiring company. In that event, if the takeover offer does not eventuate, there could be a decline in value as the stock ultimately settles down to a more normal price.

In theory, takeovers should be beneficial to the company making the takeover offer. In some cases it has worked out that way, but there have been many cases where the company taking over has not achieved the benefits it expected from the takeover situation.

28

Investing in Real Estate—
General Principles

Real estate investments, like common stocks, are an equity investment involving ownership, variable income, and capital value in contrast to the fixed returns and contractual obligation to repay capital in loan or fixed interest investments. Hence, the comments in the earlier chapters about the features of equity investments, the principles of relativity, and relative cost are applicable to this type of investment. Perhaps the best introduction to this subject is to compare real estate investments with common stocks.

Advantages of Real Estate Compared with Common Stocks

Perhaps the most significant advantage of real estate investment compared with common stocks is that real estate gives the investor a far greater degree of control over the results of his or her investments. Decisions made by the investor on the management of the property invested in provide far greater control for the investor than in common stocks, where the results of the investment may depend to a considerable extent on decisions made by directors of companies (directors over which all investors except those with considerable amounts of capital have little direct control).

Many investors prefer real estate because it gives them an opportunity to use their knowledge of particular localities close to where they work or live or other areas in which they are particularly interested and to exercise their judgment as to the areas most likely to prosper.

For all investors except those who pay little or no tax, real estate investment in the United States provides significant tax benefits. One is the deduction of interest on funds borrowed, which can provide the leverage or multiplication effect discussed in Chapter 15. Interest cost can reduce the income subject to normal taxation at a relatively high rate for many investors, while the borrowing increases the capital gain taxed at a lower rate generally some years later, further reducing the effective cost. (Borrowing can also be used for other investments, but it is more appropriate and funds are generally more readily available for real estate.)

Accelerated depreciation allowances and other means of achieving tax benefits through the way in which property investments are structured can increase the tax benefits.

In the past, real estate investment, especially income-producing investment, has generally tended to be more stable, though there are market fluctuations. These markets are generally not as volatile as those for common stock. (It is possible that real estate markets may become more volatile in the future than in the past because of the increase in the relative cost of these investments and the gap between income yield and the yield available on other investments.)

Disadvantages Compared with Common Stock

For many investors with small to moderate amounts of capital available, one serious disadvantage of direct investment in property is that it is difficult to obtain a sufficient spread over different investments in the interests of not having "too many eggs in one basket." One property investment, even with the use of some borrowed funds, may represent a major part of the investor's capital. A somewhat allied disadvantage is the fact that, generally, property investments are not easily divisible. Investors in common stock can "fine tune" their portfolios by selling, if so desired, a relatively small percentage of their holdings. But the person who has invested in real estate generally cannot readily sell a small part of the investment, as it is usually a case of sell the whole investment or hold it. These two disadvantages of lack of spread of investment and the fact that it is not easily divisible can be overcome by the investor who does not invest directly, but invests by way of a real estate investment trust or similar arrangement. (See comments in a later chapter.)

Another disadvantage is that trends in property markets are not so obvious. Because there is not one centralized market with indexes to measure price changes which are available in the stock market, real estate investors do not have information on trends in the property markets. This has caused some painful surprises to investors forced to face a significant loss by selling in an adverse market.

Market Cycles in Real Estate

"I don't like paper markets such as stocks and shares because they fluctuate too much. That's why I invest in real estate—in good old solid bricks and mortar." That comment and the statement that real estate values must rise because replacement costs of buildings increase due to inflation are often made by investors. Both statements appear to make sense at first sight but are really two dangerous fallacies which have caused many investors to lose money.

The first statement is incorrect because both real estate and stock markets have one thing in common: they are subject to cyclical movements; booms and busts; and times when changes in market sentiment, excessive enthusiasm, or a severe reaction from earlier enthusiasm can have more effect on the results of an investment than what is happening in the company, in the case of common stocks, or the fortunes of a particular property, in the case of real estate investment.

The second statement, that rising costs will ensure a steady increase in real estate values, would only be true if values were set by some formula related to cost. In fact, values are determined by supply and demand. There have been periods in the last few years when a significant increase in replacement cost due to inflation has been accompanied not by a similar rise in property values but by a decline in property values resulting from oversupply.

Indicators of Imminent Slumps

Though real estate markets generally tend to be less volatile than stock markets, they are subject to cyclical movements. There are some signs of possible imminent decline in real estate markets which investors should remember. One is a situation of increasing money supply. This is likely to cause the monetary authorities to tighten credit, leading to increased interest rates. This, in turn, leads to difficulties by some speculators in meeting their commitments or refinancing loans negotiated earlier at much lower interest rates, which may trigger off a cyclical slump.

Another sign is unnaturally rapid development in areas away from those where development could be logically expected—that is, an orderly progression from city center to meet the needs of greater population. An acceleration in the rate of increase in prices is another sign that the end of the boom and a significant cyclical slump may not be far away. If prices plotted on a chart show an almost vertical movement well above what could be expected to be the normal trading range (see comments in other chapters), then the slump may be fairly close.

More than usual advertising of particular types of property, or developers giving interest concessions (i.e., charging a rate lower than the going rate at that time or "buying down" mortgages), are other signs of a cyclical slump. So too are high relative costs, in other words, a large and growing gap between the income return on real estate investments and the cost of borrowing or the returns available on fixed interest investments.

Indicators of Possible Recovery

Signs that a recovery is starting or is about to start would involve circumstances almost directly opposite to those outlined above.

Investors for Whom Real Estate Is Suitable

Income-producing real estate is a medium risk investment because of market fluctuation. Vacant land or land producing a very low income pending redevelopment is generally in the high risk category, producing very good results in favorable conditions and poor results for serious losses in adverse conditions. For these reasons, real estate investment is not suitable for the person who must adopt a very low risk investment policy—the person with limited funds, or limited income from other sources, a person who is getting on in years, retired, or dependent on investments for all or most of his or her income.

It is a suitable investment for those who can adopt a medium or high risk policy for at least a portion of their funds. For many of those people who may be paying a relatively high rate of tax, the tax benefits referred to earlier in the chapter might make it particularly attractive.

The fact that any single investment in real estate tends to be of fairly significant amount could provide problems for some investors with small to moderate amounts available for investment if they wish to limit the amount in any one investment to a reasonable proportion of their total funds. Investments through real estate investment trust, discussed in a later chapter, may be an alternative.

Crucial Factors in Real Estate Investment

Some real estate people say that there are three rules for real estate investment. Of those three rules, the first is location, the second is location, and the third is location. It is true that location is important, but so too is timing. In times of cyclical slump, even the best located property may decline considerably in value. So it is important to consider the facts as discussed earlier in this chapter, including relative costs and the current position of the market cycle, in timing the purchase or sale of real estate investments.

Another factor is the ease of management. For this reason, many real estate investors prefer commercial or industrial investment rather than residential. Investment in residential real estate sometimes tends to produce more problems in terms of management, especially with the small percentage of tenants who may be somewhat irresponsible. The use of a good managing agent can reduce but not entirely eliminate these problems. Commercial investment where the tenant is one or a few established businesses tends to minimize management problems.

The Place of Borrowing in Real Estate Investment

The idea of borrowing, within prudent limits, to make possible participation in investments that would otherwise not be available, or to invest earlier than would otherwise be possible, is not limited to real estate investments. However, borrowing is more readily applicable in this type of investment, partly because funds are more readily available at reasonable cost for real estate investments than for other more volatile investments such as common stocks. The advent of mortgage insurance in the last few decades has also increased the scope for borrowing.

In general, it is wise to consider the principles in relation to borrowing in Chapter 15. These are recognizing the way in which borrowing increases the risk of an investment; the need to limit liabilities to a reasonable portion of net worth; to see that cash flow from other sources such as salary or business or professional income would be adequate to meet at least part of the interest and repayment commitments if the real estate investment does not produce an adequate cash flow; the need to ensure a balanced maturity pattern for borrowings; plan borrowings carefully avoiding the difficulties of borrowing at times of high interest rates or tight money conditions; the maintenance of adequate cash reserves or access to funds through credit lines with banks or other organizations; and the need to watch more closely investments in which borrowing is involved.

Prudent borrowing has enabled many investors to build up their capital much more rapidly than otherwise would have been possible. The increase in value of housing over the last 20 years or so made a foundation for a sound investment program for many people. They commenced their significant investment by borrowing against the increasing equity in their homes (due both to the gradual repayment of their liability and, more particularly, to the rapid increase in value of the property).

Does High Relative Cost Make Real Estate Markets Vulnerable?

In Part 4, in the chapters dealing with relative cost, the point was made that the stock market in recent years has been at a very high level relative to fixed interest investments. A somewhat similar position applies in real estate investments (though specific figures are not available for those markets).

The basic fact is that the emphasis on seeking capital gain and tax shelters through real estate investments in the last 10 years or so has pushed real estate values in many areas up to levels well above what would have been considered realistic in more normal times. In earlier years, in real estate, as in stock market and other equity areas, investment could be made at prices which were realistic in relation to the earnings return and current interest rate. In recent years, the gap between the income return on real estate investments and the cost of money and returns available on fixed interest investments has widened considerably.

As indicated in an earlier chapter, this is a potential source of significant capital decline. That capital decline could occur if and when the market decided that yield gaps were too high and that it was necessary to return to the more realistic basis of earlier years. No one can say whether that change of market sentiment will take place or, if it does take place, when it is likely to occur. But the fact that it may occur does mean there is a potential source of significant decline which real estate investors together with investors in other equity areas cannot ignore.

29

Investing in Real Estate—
Some Specifics

In this chapter, we turn to look at some of the specifics of investing in real estate. All of the material in this chapter should be considered within the framework of the general comments on real estate investments, including cyclical market movements and other factors, discussed in Chapter 18. It is also necessary to consider this information within the broader framework of the comments in earlier chapters in Parts 2, 3, and 4 dealing with return, risk, and relativity, as well as the earlier chapters of Part 5 on investment policy and strategy.

Different Types of Real Estate Investments

Of the investments in real estate which produce income as well as prospects of capital gain if markets cooperate with the investor's prediction, the residential area is the one best known to most small to medium investors. It includes single-family buildings and multifamily dwellings.

In the commercial and industrial areas there are warehouses, shops, and office buildings. A recent development in this area has been the ministorage warehouses, reatively small in size, which provide storage facilities for records or other material. As office space has become more expensive to buy or rent, business people are looking for facilities such as these in which to store noncurrent files and records which would otherwise involve much more expensive space in modern office buildings.

In the nonincome-producing category (or the category where the returns are very small) are vacant land held for later sale, possibly after subdivision and redevelopment sometime in the future when changes in the zoning regulations make this possible. Sometimes it may be possible to earn a moderate income by the use of the land for growing crops or running livestock, but in general this type of investment produces a return which is very small in relation to the capital involved. If the land is vacant and not being used in any way, there is a negative income comprised of the outlays for property tax.

In deciding which of the various range of investments are suitable, each individual investor would have to see how they fit in with his or her investment policy based on one's particular financial situation and one's knowledge of the type of investment. (Many real estate investors prefer residential investment because it enables them to use their knowledge of local areas close to where they live or work.)

Another alternative is to invest indirectly through real estate investment trusts, which is discussed in a later chapter.

Points to Be Considered in Making Real Estate Investment Decisions

Set out below is a summary of the matters to be considered before making buying decisions. They would also be relevant in considering whether to continue to hold real estate investments or to consider the sale of all or part of them (if a partial sale is practicable).

Immediate Location

Does the immediate environment create a good impression? Are the buildings in the immediate vicinity attractive-looking? (There is a saying that it may be good business to buy the one somewhat unattractive house in a block of attractive houses where some minor improvements coupled with the attractive surroundings may increase value significantly.)

Are there any wrong types of buildings adjacent to the property (for example, a high quality single-family residence with apartment buildings on either side which would detract from the tone of the property)?

General Location

Is the suburb or district the right area?

Is the area a growing one in which increasing popularity for the particular type of real estate is likely to enhance values, or is it an area which is in danger of being left behind as housing or business activities move to faster-growing areas elsewhere?

Is the area likely to benefit from any current or pending improvement to roads or transport facilities or suffer from lack of adequate facilities, or become a sort of backwater as the result of freeway construction reducing the business area considerably?

Are current and likely local, regional, or national migration patterns beneficial or adverse?

Type of Property

Is the type of property suitable from the viewpoint of the following?

1. The needs and investment goals of the individual.
2. The area in which it is located.
3. The time at which the investment is being made.
4. The ease of management.

Is the property a general purpose property which could be occupied by a business other than that carried on at present in the event of the lease not being renewed, or is it a single purpose building capable of being used effectively only by one type of business?

Supply Situation

Is the supply situation at present and for the medium-term future, as far as that can be estimated, such that rental levels, rental loss through vacancies, net income, and capital values reflecting that net income would make it an attractive investment?

Is the property of the type that is subject to periodical bursts of excessive activity leading to oversupply problems, or is it one where the supply pattern is less volatile?

Does the trend in approvals for construction (which may lead commencements by some time and completion by a longer period) indicate that oversupply may not be too far away?

Demand Situation

Is there a healthy demand for that type of space in that area?

Are changing economic conditions, or the relative attractions of other areas, likely to affect demand?

If inquiries are made in the role of a potential tenant, does the number of properties available from letting agents confirm statements as to demand made by vendors or their agents?

Income Expenditure and Net Earnings

Do the figures submitted appear reasonable on the basis of inquiries as to matters discussed above?

Is there adequate provision for the following:

1. Vacancies.
2. Long-term maintenance.
3. Depreciation.

4. Repairs to damage to parking areas, courtyards, and other outside areas due to rain and storm water.
5. Management, including possible local maintenance man on some residential properties as well as managing agents.

Prospects of Maintaining and/or Increasing Rental Levels

Is the current rental level in line with the going rate so that in the event of the bankruptcy of the present tenant or failure to renew the lease there should not be too much difficulty in finding another tenant without significant rent reduction?

Are actual or emerging surpluses of accomodation in neighboring areas or in similar but not identical accomodation likely to spill over into this area or this type of property?

Physical Condition of the Property

Can the physical soundness of the property be verified by reference to architectural or engineering specialists?

Are there any problems in relation to the site? For example, is there subsidence on reclaimed land, possible landslips on steeply sloping sites, or erosion in farming properties?

Zoning

Is the zoning such that it will help the property to hold and enhance its value?

Are there any trends for rezoning of adjoining properties or adjoining areas which could affect the popularity of the particular property or properties in that area?

Market Value and Replacement Cost

How does current market value compare with replacement cost of the property? (Though the fact that market value is below current replacement costs or expected replacement costs a few years hence does not ensure that market values will be maintained or increased, a situation where market value is clearly well above replacement costs could be dangerous.)

Relative Cost

How does the cost of the property relative to fixed interest investment returns compare with other equity investments and the relative cost of this type of investment in the past?

Sensitivity Analysis

How significant would changes in some of the crucial variables, such as vacancies, rental levels, and management costs, be on the expected returns?

Purchase of Property for Improvement

Some investors have done very well in real estate through purchase of properties which offer scope for improvement. They may be properties that are well below their potential earning capacity because of bad management, because they have been allowed to drift into a state of disrepair, or because they are not providing the facilities that are available from other properties competing for the same type of tenant. Investors who have some skill in, or knowledge of, trades such as building, plumbing, electrical work, and so on, may be able to utilize their skills in this way. Other people without those technical skills may also do well in this area if they have experience in arranging for this work to be done effectively and economically by reliable tradespeople.

As well as providing scope for increased income, this sort of operation, if it is handled properly, may also provide better than average normal scope for capital gain. The reason is that the improved earning capacity should be reflected in enhanced capital value for the property. These investments may also provide better than normal tax benefits because at least some of the expenditure of repairing the property is an allowable deduction from taxable income and also helps to increase the capital gain, generally taxed at a lower rate and at some time in the future.

The key to this sort of operation is to ensure that the expenditure on repairs and improvements is obvious to prospective tenants or buyers of the property. Sometimes repairs or improvements which are little more than cosmetic in nature may provide a better return for the investor than more comprehensive changes.

Tax Benefits from Real Estate Investment

In deciding which investment is suitable for a particular investor, the tax benefits may often be a significant factor. Obviously, the person who is earning a higher income and hence facing a higher rate of income tax would be more attracted to the real estate investment which provides better tax benefits—possibly through borrowing to produce a deduction from other income of the interest costs, which may exceed the revenue of the property, and multiply the capital gain, on which tax is not payable for some time until the property is sold and then generally at a rate much lower than the normal income tax rate for many taxpayers. In deciding which type of investment is most suitable, investors seeking tax benefits may have a preference for those which provide scope for the use of accelerated depreciation allowances.

Possible Traps in Sale and Lease Back Arrangements

Sometimes the owner of a property may wish to sell it to free capital for use in other ways and then lease back the property from the new owner. Sometimes these deals are arranged on the basis that the new owner receives an agreed rate of return, being his net income, with the lessee (the former owner) paying all outgoings.

A trap for the unwary in this type of deal is to buy on the basis of a good initial return without checking to see whether the total rent paid by the lessee (the net return to the owner plus the outgoings) is in line with the going rate for similar accommodation. If it is well above the going rate, there could be serious problems if the lessee later gets into financial difficulties or if the lease is not renewed. In that event, the new owner may face both reduced income and a significant capital loss, or at least much lower capital gain than he or she expected.

Often owners suggesting a sale and lease back arrangement will offer to pay a rental much above the going rate. It may suit them to do this because the higher the rent which they are prepared to pay, the higher the capital sum they receive from the purchaser on the basis of an agreed income return. For the original owner in that situation, there is also a tax benefit in paying a higher rent. The higher rent paid would normally be tax deductible, but the additional price paid for sale of the building because of that higher rental would generally be a capital gain, on which the tax rate would normally be lower.

Sensitivity Analysis—Example

An example of the sensitivity analysis which is included among the matters to be considered before making investment decisions (or in reviewing investments) is included as an appendix to Chapter 16.

30

Gold, Silver, Futures Trading, Options, and Other Investments

Gold

The investor who purchased gold at the low point in October 1976, around $105 per ounce, and sold in January 1980 at about $850 per ounce enjoyed a gain of 710 percent in about three and a quarter years. That works out at 90 percent per annum compound, a rate of gain matched by few other investments. But for the person who purchased at the peak in 1980 and sold at a low point in 1983 at $297, there was a loss of about 67 percent, or two thirds of the investment, in a little over three years (in addition to the cost of insurance and storage and the significant opportunity cost of the loss of income which could have been earned on other investments). The vast contrast in the results of those two periods dramatically illustrates that there is a high degree of risk involved in investments in gold.

To a considerable extent, the other investments discussed in this chapter—silver, futures trading, options, and some other investments— are also in the high risk category. Hence, these investments generally are not suitable for investors with limited capital, low or uncertain income from other sources, or those for whom a low risk investment policy is appropriate. Even those who can afford a medium or high risk policy should take the precaution of limiting the portion of their total capital in these investments to a relatively small percentage.

In the heady days of 1979–80 when gold prices were rising so rapidly, we were told by many enthusiasts, and not a few investment specialists who should have known better, that gold was the ultimate store of value and a sure hedge against inflation. Neither of those statements is valid. Remember the point made in an earlier chapter that no investment provides an automatic or assured hedge against inflation because, as Abraham Lincoln pointed out, you cannot fool all of the people all of the time.

One of the great advantages of gold is that it is highly portable. In crisis situations such as wars or revolutions, refugees can take a considerable amount of capital with them in pocket or purse or small container if it is in the form of gold. Because it has long been used as part of the monetary system (though to a lesser extent in recent years), it has advantages that do not apply to other commodities. The fact that central banks of most countries continue to keep a portion of their reserves in gold is another favorable factor.

On the other hand, the experience of recent years has shown that gold cannot resist the law of gravity. Speculative booms such as that at the end of the 1970s can be followed by a severe decline in price and a long period before complete recovery. The fact that at the beginning of 1984 the gold price of around $380 was more than 50 percent below the peak of four years earlier is very significant. This is the first time in 50 years that gold has experienced such a severe and prolonged decline. For almost 40 years the price was fixed. In the 10 years or so since the end of that era, the longest previous slump was about 2 years between 1974 and 1976.

The higher interest rates of the late 70s and 80s are another adverse factor. Simply to break even with other investments which provide income, gold would have to increase in price at a much higher rate now than in the days of low interest rates (except to the extent that for some investors tax on high-yielding investments reduces the gap). Another significant point is that in the early 80s, gold prices failed to recover to 1980 levels despite severe international tension in areas such as Iran, Afghanistan, Poland, and Lebanon, as well as pressures on the international monetary system through difficulties in debtor nations such as Brazil, Argentina, Mexico, and Poland.

Because of the large amount of speculation in gold markets, timing is essential, and success really goes to those who can best judge the short-term mood of the market and take advantage of short-term swings.

Possible Normal Trading Range for Gold

In an earlier chapter there was a reference to estimating normal trading range as one way of considering the general area in which prices may be expected in later years. It is not a precise means of estimating future prices, but it is useful as a means of indicating the area where, on the balance of probabilities, prices could be expected in the future. This is certainly a useful exercise in resisting the claims that gold or any other market is likely to reach very high figures a few years hence.

An example of the use of the normal trading range may be of interest.

Early in 1981, many people were predicting that in the next two years or so prices would increase to $1,000 or beyond. The chart I prepared then to estimate probable normal range indicated that at the end of 1982, the gold price would probably be in the range of $350 to $470. As it turned out, the price of gold at the end of 1982 was around $425. Let me stress that this successful example does not mean that there is any magic about this approach. It is a reasonable, sensible way of making some sort of systematic approach to estimating the general area of future prices.

Chart 30–1 shows an estimated normal trading range for gold. This chart was prepared early in 1983. The base line of the normal trading range was the upward trend line from the November 1978 low point to the June 1982 low point. That line indicated a rise at the rate of about 13 percent per annum compound. The top of the normal range is a line parallel to the upward trend line at a level which would indicate peaks in the normal range about 20 percent above the midpoint of the range, with the base line about 20 percent below that midpoint. You can see from the chart that in the period of about five years, prices were within that range for most of the time with the exception of the rapid rise in the boom of 1979–80 and the reaction to that boom in 1980–81.

You can see from the chart that the normal trading range for February 1984 would be the range from $370 to $580. It turned out that in February 1984, about a year after this normal trading range was estimated, prices were about that base line figure of $380 (though signs of weakness in the market gave some indication that it could decline below

Chart 30–1

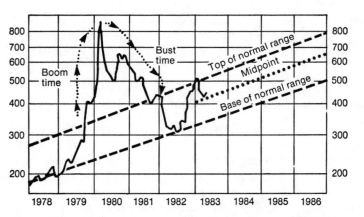

that level). At the time of preparing the estimated normal trading range, my comment was that if prices were to decline a little lower, to about $400, then gold could be bought with more confidence than for most of the time in the previous four years when it had either been in the top section of the normal range or well above it in the late 1979 to late 1981 period.

In the year after that estimate was made, prices declined a little further to around $380. It remains to be seen whether subsequent movement would justify that cautious suggestion for some buying around $400. One of the values of estimating the normal range was the associated suggestion that investors should be prepared to take a profit by selling at least some of their holdings of gold (or their investment in gold futures when prices moved into the upper section of the normal trading range, i.e., above $500 to $550 in mid-1984).

Inability of Markets to Maintain Steeply Rising Trends

In Chapter 24, the point was made that if prices are rising at a moderate rate, that rising trend may be maintained for a long period, but if they are rising sharply, that trend is not likely to be maintained for long. As a general rule, few markets have been able to maintain in the longer term of 5 to 10 years or more, a rate of increase in prices above 10 to 15 percent per annum compound.

It is worth noting that the very long-term upward trend in common stocks as measured by the Dow Jones Industrial Index from the low point of 41 in July 1932 to the low point of 776 in August 1982 works out at 6.0 percent per annum compound. It is this fact that tends to make the estimation of normal trading range helpful in considering future price movements.

Silver

In earlier times, silver also had a place in the monetary system, particularly in coins. In the latter years of the last century and the early years of this century, there was a strong lobby for the idea of bimetallism, which would have involved the use of silver as well as gold in the standard on which U.S. currency was based. In support of the plank providing for bimetallism in the Democratic party platform, William Jennings Bryan made his celebrated "cross of gold" speech at the 1896 convention in Chicago including the statement, "you shall not crucify mankind upon a cross of gold."

Silver is not used so extensively in coins now because rising prices have made it necessary for many countries to use cupro-nickel rather than silver in coins of low value. One interesting aspect of production of silver which many see as an advdantage in relation to its price is that most silver is produced more or less as a by-product in mines where the main activity is the production of lead, copper, or gold. There is an argument that this makes silver prices less volatile than those of other metals because a rise in the price of silver does not lead to the big increase in production which follows when prices of other metals rise. Hence, the argument goes, silver is not exposed to the rapid declines which follow overproduction.

There is still some validity in that argument, but it has perhaps been overwhelmed by the increase in speculation in silver in recent years. It is this speculation which produced a sevenfold increase in price in 1979–80 and a decline of about 85 percent in the next two years. At that time, losses to some speculators might have caused serious financial problems for some dealers and other sections of the financial sector of the U.S. economy and a domino-like effect, had special finance not been made available to cover the emergency. Rapid growth in electronics and photography, which are among the major uses of silver, has helped to support prices in the last few decades.

Between mid-1982, the low point after the long decline from the early 1980 peak, to early 1983, the price of silver showed a threefold increase that would have made those who bought silver at the low point very happy. Since then, the market has moved in a fairly indefinite way. As with gold or any other commodities, success in this market depends to a considerable extent on gauging the mood of the market, the momentum of rising or falling trends, and associated factors.

Futures Trading in Commodities and Financial Packages

For many years, futures markets have provided the means for investors and others to back their judgments about a future price trend without having to become involved in physically buying and selling the relevant items. Those who felt prices were likely to rise would buy futures contracts for delivery or settlement at some future date, generally in the range of 3 to 18 months ahead. Those who felt that prices were about to decline could sell a futures contract giving them the right to sell at a selected future date within the range covered by the futures contract. If the market cooperated with their predictions, they would benefit by the extent of the difference between the price at which they bought or sold and the current or "spot" price at the future date (the buyer being able to exercise his or her right to buy at the lower price prevailing when he/she bought the forward contract, and the seller, in the event of prices going down as he/she predicted, being able to sell at the higher price prevailing when he/she sold forward).

In addition to a number of commodities of various kinds on which futures trading is possible, a number of financial futures have been introduced in recent years. These include futures related to common stock indexes, interest rate futures, or futures related to the value of currencies.

Using Futures Markets to Hedge

One of the uses of futures markets, which some would see as the more conservative use of them, is to hedge against the uncertainty of future prices. For example, producers of commodities who fear that prices may decline during the next few months before their commodity is ready for the market may sell for forward delivery at today's price. If, as they expected, prices decline, then they can exercise their right to sell at the later date at the high price at which the forward contract was negotiated. Or more frequently, they may sell in the normal course through regular market channels and then close out their futures contract by buying a similar contract with the same expiration date and price. In that event, the difference between the lower price at which they close out or buy their forward contract and the higher price at which they earlier sold it offsets the difference in the physical market between the price at which they sell and the price prevailing sometime earlier. Thus, they have in effect locked in the benefit of the higher price prevailing at the earlier period except for the relatively small cost of dealing in the futures market. In financial futures, hedging operations may be used to protect against the risk of a fall or rise in interest rates, value of currencies, or stock market indices.

Trading or Speculating in Futures

The other basic use of futures markets is for trading or speculation. For the person who has the capital, time, skills, and temperament for speculating and backing his or her judgment about future price trends, futures markets may often be more attractive than the commodity markets themselves. One reason is that in the futures market the initial outlay is generally a small percentage, perhaps around 5 to 10 percent, of the value of the contract for the underlying commodities. This enables a trader to "speculate on margins" enjoying a leverage effect, so that a 10 percent rise in the price of a commodity may yield a 100 percent rise on the investment if the deposit was 10 percent.

Such a person, of course, has to accept the fact that the leverage also increases the risk, because there is a multiplying effect if the market goes contrary to his or her predictions. If the market moves against him or her, he/she may soon receive margin calls, which means that he/she has to pay to the broker or dealer amounts related to the decline in the market if he/she has bought forward (expecting prices to rise) and a rise in the market if he/she has sold forward (expecting a fall).

Some Basic Principles for Futures Trading

They used to say in the army that the first thing to do in cleaning a rifle was to check the number to make sure you didn't clean the rifle belonging to someone else by mistake. In futures trading, perhaps the first thing for any investor to consider is whether he or she should be in that market. It is obviously not a market in which you invest next week's housekeeping money or money needed for educational expenses or other essential items. In general, it is a market for those with a reasonable amount of capital who could afford to place a portion of it in the high risk market so that if things turn out badly and they suffer a severe loss of that part of their capital, it does not have a major effect on their cash position or overall financial situation.

The other major principles which could be applied would be summarized as follows:

1. Limit total commitment in this type of high risk operation to about 10 percent of funds available for investment (not of total capital including home and business assets, but 10 percent of more or less liquid funds available for investment).
2. Remember that this is one area in which time does not cure all ills, because futures contracts expire on a certain date. If you prediction of the future direction of the market is correct but it does not start to move in the right direction until after the expiration of the period covered by your forward contract, that is too bad. (You do not have the option as you do when you buy stock or real estate of riding out a downturn and waiting for a subsequent recovery).
3. Apply the general principle of cutting losses and trying to let profits run.
4. As a significant number of your operations are likely to produce losses, even if your overall operations are profitable, limit your

initial investment to about 10 percent of the total which you plan to commit in this area.

5. If the market cooperates with your predictions, make additional investments of a smaller size (For example, make five contracts in the first investment, four in the second, three in the third, etc. This would mean that in the event of a sudden turn in the market, you are not likely to be caught with such heavy losses on recently made investments).

6. Use stop orders to limit losses and preserve profits. (Stop orders are orders that take effect when the market reaches a certain level.)

7. Select carefully the broker or dealer with whom you transact your business and develop a good working relationship with him or her.

8. Consider fundamentals such as weather conditions, supply and demand, effect of currency changes (and also technical factors such as support and resistance, trend movements, momentum of the market).

9. Consider the use of spread trading. A spread involves the taking of simultaneous positions aimed to counterbalance each other, for example, long and short positions in a commodity in different months or different markets, or different commodities which are related. The key to this trading is the difference between the prices of the original positions, so that profits may be made not from the actual rise and decline in the market but the way in which those changes affect the spread between the initial positions.

Options on Futures Contracts

An option on a futures contract enables the option holder to buy or sell a futures contract at an agreed price within an agreed period. These options could appeal to the investor who wishes to operate in the futures market but to limit downside risk. Normal futures market trading can have virtually an open ended risk through the combination of very sharp movements in underlying commodity prices, such as gold or silver in 1979–80, and the leverage or multiplying effect resulting from the initial deposit being a small percentage of the contract value.

In normal futures operations, those two factors could mean that the ultimate loss could be many times the amount of the initial investment of the deposit on the contract. On the other hand, the investor who purchases an option knows that his or her investment can never exceed more than the cost of that option. If the market completely fails to cooperate with his or her predictions, he/she does not exercise the option and loses only the cost of the option. Naturally, this limiting of the downside risk also means that in the event of the market cooperating with one's predictions, one's gain would not be as great as if one operated in the futures market directly. But it could appeal to many investors who wish to keep downside risk to a known and limited amount.

Options on Listed Stocks

It is also possible to buy options on listed stocks. A *call option* is an option which gives the holder the right to purchase stock at an agreed exercise price up to the end of a specified period. A *put option* is an option which enables the holder to sell stock at an agreed exercise price up to a specified date. Investors who have a particular stock in their portfolio may feel that it is overpriced but may hestitate to sell it because of uncertainty about future price trends. In that event, they could buy a put option which gives them the right to sell the stock at the current price over a certain period. If the stock price subsequently declines considerably, they would be able to sell at the higher price specified in the put contract. They would thus be better off to the extent of the difference between the earlier price when the put option was bought and the later price minus the cost of buying the put. (To that extent the cost of the put option and the cost of dealing are a sort of insurance premium against a larger fall.)

Some holders of stocks decide to write options, that is, to sell them as a means of increasing the return of the portfolio. If they write or sell a call option and the stock subsequently increases greatly in price, then obviously the option would be exercised by the buyer. The original holder would then have received the premium or payment for the call option plus the lower price prevailing at the time the option was written. He or she would miss out on the larger gain that would have been available if he/she had not written the option.

On the other hand, the holder receives the amount for the call option which is actual money. It may often happen that the option one writes is not exercised because the stock does not rise sufficiently to justify it, or in fact the stock may fall. So investors see this as a means of increasing their overall return, knowing that they may give up the chance of some very large gains in exchange for a lower and more definite overall return.

From the viewpoint of the trader, the purchase of a call option provides a means of speculating on margins similar to operating in the futures market. The call options may also be used by a person who wishes to buy stock but is unable to do so at present because funds are not yet available. In that event, one may consider it good business to buy a call option and lock oneself into the current price which one expects to be lower than that prevailing some months later when funds are available to make the purchase.

There are other refinements of options trading, including the use of straddles, involving a call and put option for more experienced operators in this market.

Further Information on Futures and Options Trading

A number of the larger brokerage houses have publications and information in relation to the operations described in this chapter. I have found the "Merrill Lynch Guide to Speculating in Commodity Futures" a useful publication. It discusses various aspects of trading in commodity futures and principles to be applied in a way which can readily be understood. Merrill Lynch also has a number of other publications dealing with particular aspects of the question, such as technical analysis related to futures trading, computerized trading techniques, relative strength indicators, and economic models for some commodity prices, as well as an explanation and application of contrary opinion indicators.

Collectibles

In recent years, a number of investors have been attracted to what are sometimes called collectibles and sometimes called tangible investments. They include art, stamps, Persian carpets, antique furniture, coins, vintage automobiles—indeed, any item that may offer prospects of an increase in value. Diamonds are another example of this type of investment.

Those who buy when prices are relatively low and sell when they are high may do very well out of these investments. But for others, the result can be disappointing and may involve substantial loss. In this area, investors should be wary of confidently made claims that there is some special feature about a particular type of investment which protects it from serious downside risk. For example, it used to be said that diamonds had little or no downside risk because the diamond market was controlled to a considerable extent by major South African interests, and this control prevented the market from having the volatile movements common in other commodity and investment markets. Just how far this statement was from the facts was dramatically illustrated by stories in the late 1970s of well-known investors, including some Hollywood personalities, whose diamond investments were most disappointing.

For some people, this type of investment has an additional advantage in that they derive some pleasure out of holding the investments as well as the ultimate financial result. For example, a person who enjoys having paintings or other art objects in his or her home may consider that even if the investment results are disappointing, they are worthwhile having for the pleasure they provide. (A cynic has said that if you invest in art and the prices do not move the way you hoped they would, you can then explain you are not one of these philistines who invest in art for financial gain and tell everyone how much pleasure you obtain from looking at the painting or art objects—which is more than you can say about contemplating the beauties of a stock or bond certificate.)

Investment in collectibles makes more sense to people who have some interest in the particular area, or perhaps have been hobby collectors. Those people are more likely to do well in this type of investment because of their background knowledge. For other people going into the investment, they should be well aware of a couple of major points. One is that the margin or spread between buying and selling prices may be as much as 50 percent or more. This means that there may need to be a substantial increase in value to produce any net gain of significance. Another point is that if you do not have knowledge of the particular area yourself, you would need to make sure you have the advice of a specialist who would have your interests at heart and not simply be intent on making profit from selling collectibles to you.

31

Managing Your Investments— Do It Yourself or Delegate to a Specialist?

In the last few chapters, we have looked at a number of different types of investments ranging from low risk fixed interest investments through common stocks and property investments to gold, silver, futures trading, options, and collectibles. We now turn to the question of management of investments and the alternative of self-management or delegation of this task to a specialist.

The Need for Management

There is no such thing as a portfolio which manages itself. However carefully the portfolio may have been selected, it has to be managed effectively. Over time, the attraction of various investments changes. So too do the investment needs and policy requirements of investors. Some of these points were discussed in Chapter 16.

In equity investments such as common stocks or property, there is a constant need to consider questions such as the merits of selling to preserve profits or cut losses, a change in composition of the portfolio to meet changing conditions, the need to sell or at least reduce holdings in stocks or industries which may be facing imminent problems, and the need to reduce holdings in particular stocks or in the stock market or real estate market before the commencement of the inevitable reaction to previous rapid price rises.

For fixed interest investments the need for management is not quite so extensive, but these portfolios should not be left completely without attention. Apart from reviewing the credit-worthiness of the companies in which funds have been invested, there is a need to consider matters such as the merits of shortening or lengthening the average period to maturity.

In general, if it appeared that interest rates were likely to rise, there would be merits in shortening the portfolio, holding new money in very short-term investments with the idea of making medium- to long-term investments later when interest rates are higher. If interest rates were likely to decline significantly, there would be merit in lengthening the average period to maturity or perhaps using short-term borrowings to take advantage of higher rates before the decline in interest rates commences. (Remember the basic point made in earlier chapters that in longer term investments the risk is greater because the effect of any subsequent increase in interest rates is more significant in relation to the capital value of those investments than investments with a shorter period to maturity.)

The Pros and Cons of Delegation to Specialists

One of the advantages of delegating investment management to specialists is the same as that achieved in using specialist expertise in other areas: the use of expertise in investment management which most individual investors would lack. Even those with the knowledge and skill in financial and market matters may lack the research facilities and information which is available to specialists.

Another advantage is the spread of investment provided through investment in mutual funds or real estate investment trusts if that avenue of delegation is used. Generally, those organizations have a more or less continuing cash flow which helps investment management by diverting new funds into other areas. These organizations can reduce the proportion of the portfolio in a market that is experiencing problems. That avenue is not available to many individual investors, who do not have a continuing flow of funds available for investment.

An associated advantage of delegation to specialists is that individuals are freed of the worry of deciding what to do and also the chores of handling dividend checks and other paperwork. This can be a considerable advantage, particularly for investors who may take extended trips to foreign countries, long vacations, or become involved in high pressure situations at business or at home through family illness or other problems.

Of the disadvantages of delegating to specialists, some investors would believe the cost of these services is a disadvantage. Others would see the cost as a reasonable payment for the expertise provided and, in the case of mutual funds, a sort of insurance premium for the greater safety that should be available through the wider spread as well as the investment expertise. For some investors, the delegation to specialists would deprive them of the task of keeping up-to-date with market trends, which many people find interesting and challenging (generally more interesting and more enjoyable if not more challenging when the market is going the right way).

Another disadvantage of delegation is that, unfortunately, some specialists and mutual fund managers do not provide a sufficiently high standard of professional management. The point has been made in earlier chapters that mutual fund managers, in common with some other investment institutions, sometimes suffer from the selling tail wagging the investment dog. They succumb to the temptation of seeking the best short-term performance through undue concentration in more volatile sections of the market. This is great in the short term, especially for the sales people, but often turns out to be against the medium- and long-term interests of the investors.

The Range of Facilities Available

In considering the management of portfolios, investors have the following three broad alternatives open to them:

1. To manage the portfolio themselves, perhaps initially with advice from investment specialists in setting up the portfolio and in periodic reviews of the portfolio (perhaps assisted by subscriptions to one or more of the large number of investment newsletters which are available).
2. Delegate the whole of the management of the portfolio to an organization of professional portfolio managers who would be given the discretion on day-by-day investment decisions, perhaps within broad policy guidelines laid down by the investor in consultation with the manager at the commencement of the arrangement.
3. Investment in mutual funds or real estate investment trusts.

Of the above alternatives, the second, the delegation to portfolio managers, would not be available for investors with smaller amounts of capital or medium and larger sums. This avenue is as economical for medium to large portfolios as the yearly fees are generally in the vicinity of about 1 percent of the value of the portfolio, or sometimes a smaller percentage. But for smaller investors in the range of a few thousand up to about the $50,000 to $100,000 range, the minimum fee which portfolio managers would have to charge would tend to work out at a rather large percentage of the relatively small amount of capital.

Range of Mutual Funds and Real Estate Investment Trusts

The several hundred mutual funds available to American investors include many different types of investment. There are some which invest in bonds, others which invest in common stocks or convertible securities. Within the common stock investment area there are mutual funds with many different objectives. Some seek maximum capital gain with relatively low income; others aim for a reasonable income and some capital gain. There are mutual funds which concentrate in particular industries or types of investment to provide a vehicle for those who prefer that particular section of the market.

For example, Sci/Tech Holdings, Inc. is a mutual fund seeking long-term capital appreciation through worldwide investment in equity securities of companies that in the opinion of management (Merrill Lynch Asset Management, Inc.) derive or are expected to derive a substantial portion of their sales from products and services in science or technology. Another mutual fund offered by the Merrill Lynch group is the Merrill Lynch Basic Value Fund, Inc., which seeks capital appreciation and, secondly, income by investing in securities, primarily equities that the management of the fund believes are undervalued and therefore represent basic investment value.

Some funds concentrate on investments in particular areas. For example, the Merrill Lynch Pacific Fund, Inc. seeks long-term capital appreciation primarily through investment in equities for corporations based in far eastern or western Pacific countries, including Japan, Australia, Hong Kong, Singapore, and the Phillippines.

Real estate investment trusts apply the principle of pooling of funds of a large number of individuals for investment in the real estate industry. Some concentrate on investment in mortgages to provide a high income, while others invest in equity position in real estate with the aim of producing a low income with prospects of capital gain.

Selection of Investment Manager or Mutual Fund

Between 1978 and 1983, many investors in mutual funds did particularly well, with total gain over that period exceeding 200 percent for a number of mutual funds. But for much of the 70s, results were disappointing, and many investors suffered substantial capital loss. In the real estate investment trust industry, declines of 50 to 80 percent in the mid-70s were common. The experience of investors who delegate their portfolio management to specialists has also varied greatly from manager to manager and from period to period.

So investors need to realize that contrary to the enthusiastic claims of some sales people, delegation of investment management does not automatically ensure good results. It is necessary to be very careful in selecting the investment manager or the mutual fund to which your funds will be entrusted.

In order to attract business, some portfolio managers, mutual funds, and real estate investment trusts are inclined to quote results for periods which are favorable to them and ignore results for other periods where the picture may have been completely different. For this reason, investors should obtain, and verify as far as possible, performance figures over a long period, preferably 10 to 15 years, as well as analyze the results over shorter periods within that overall time. They should also see whether the manager showed some professional skills in a least reducing their holding before cyclical declines. More effient managers with a professional approach, rather than a selling approach of maximizing short-term results, would have gradually reduced their holdings in market areas after prices had risen considerably. Failure to do that generally indicates that the manager is more concerned with maximizing short-term results which can be highlighted in sales presentations than concentrating on the medium- and long-term results.

Investors should also read annual reports, prospectuses, and other material to see if the investment philosophy to which the managers subscribe appears logical and objective. They should be particularly wary of portfolio managers of mutual funds that still present very confident assertions based on fallacies—for example, fallacies such as the claim that shares keep pace with inflation, that growth stocks provide assured large capital gain, or that good results in particular industries such as new "hi-tech" industries will automatically mean good results for investors. (The investors' results could be quite different if future benefits have already been overanticipated in excessive market prices.)

32

Investment Aspects of Buying a Home

For most people, the single most important investment decision they make is the purchase of their home. For many people in the last 20 or 30 years, the purchase of a home has turned out to be their most successful investment decision, though their major motives in buying the home may have been for reasons other than seeking a good investment.

The Major Investment Attractions of Investing Money in a Home

Among the major attractions of investing money in a home (or condominium) are the following:

1. The purchase of a home provides many benefits not available from other types of investments, such as the pride of ownership, the security of tenure, the freedom from worry of the tenant that the owner may sell the house and force him or her to move, the satisfaction of improving the home and yard, and a general feeling of well-being associated with home ownership.
2. The leverage benefits of a multiplication of capital gain, because a major part of the purchase price can normally be obtained through borrowed funds at relatively reasonable rates.
3. The benefit of being a long-term borrower in times of inflation with a portion of the debt being paid off in currency of lower real value in terms of purchasing power 10, 15, or 20 years after the purchase of the home.
4. Substantial taxation benefits including both the ability to deduct interests costs from income from other sources and the fact that the earnings of the investment the "imputed" income consisting of the savings compared with rental payments that would otherwise have to be made) are not taxable.

5. For most investors, a greater knowledge of this investment area than other types of investment, because most people can fairly easily acquire some knowledge of real estate trends in particular local areas in which they are interested.

If asked to define the serious disadvantages of investing money in the purchase of a home, a person may note the fact that because of the above advantages and emphasis on investment in housing for tax benefits and to combat inflation, the relative cost of homes (in terms of their earning capacity and potential rental proposition) compared with interest rates and returns on fixed interest investments has increased significantly in recent years. Another possible disadvantage is that the popularity of investment in homes sometimes leads people to overcommit themselves, partly because of social pressures to "keep up with the Joneses."

On balance, for most people at most times, the advantages of investing in a home (including the nonfinancial benefits referred to above) considerably outweigh the disadvantages. For that reason, most people try to buy a home at the first available opportunity. Generally this makes good sense, provided they go about it in the right way and avoid buying at the top of a boom.

Do You Buy a Newly Erected Home or a Previously Occupied Home?

Some people prefer to buy land in a position and area which they prefer and to build on it a home of their particular design. Others believe that the wide range of newly completed homes available from developers will suit their needs. A third group among those who decide to buy their homes purchase a previously occupied home or condo.

To a considerable extent, this decision may be based on what is available and on the personal preferences of the buyer. From a purely business or investment point of view, 30 years ago there may have been little choice in this matter, because the number of previously occupied homes available for sale was relatively small in relation to the large demand following the end of World War II. Today, there is a real choice, partly because of the general oversupply of housing due to changed population trends and a tapering off in the growth of the "headship ratio." That headship ratio is the ratio of the number of households to each 100 persons in the population. In the 1970s, growth in this ratio accounted for about one quarter of the average annual growth in households of 1.7 million.

As a general but by no means invariable guide, it would be fair to say that in a situation of oversupply either nationally or in local areas (including those in the northeastern parts of the United States, from which there has been significant migration in the last two decades), market values may tend to lag behind replacement costs. On the other hand, in a situation of shortage of supply and strong demand either nationally or locally (including those areas into which many migrants from other states have moved) there would be a tendency for market values of previously occupied homes or condos to be above replacement cost.

This means that in positions of oversupply such as that prevailing in the 1980s in most areas, home seekers may find a better bargain in buying a previously occupied home or condo. The reason is that in those conditions the seller, who probably bought the home some years earlier at a much lower price, is prepared to meet the market at a price below replacement cost, especially if he or she has to sell fairly quickly to finance the purchase of a home elsewhere.

If all other things are equal, including personal preferences for type of home, the economic arguments would tend to be toward buying a previously occupied unit under current conditions (except to the extent that competitive forces may force building companies to discount substantially the prices of recently erected units). On the other hand, if at some stage in the future the situation returns to the severe shortage of housing which was the rule in most parts of the United States for 20 or 30 years after World War II, better value may be obtained by buying land and building, or buying a recently erected home from a building company.

Relative Merits of Owning Compared with Renting in Current Conditions

Until fairly recently, the taxation advantages of owning a home, which were discussed earlier in the chapter, and long-term finance at low interest rates, made owning far more attractive than renting. During much of the 1970s, in real terms, as distinct from monetary terms, interest rates were negative.

The economic advantages of owning rather than renting are not likely to disappear overnight, but there have been many changes in recent years, which could be accentuated in the future, that may reduce the advantages of buying considerably. One of these is that the combination of substantial increase in the cost of housing and much higher interest rates have increased the cost of financing a home. In 1972 the average cost to service conventional first mortgages was about 20 percent of the average annual disposable income per household. Some years earlier it was an even smaller percentage. Ten years later, in 1982, the cost had doubled from around 20 percent to 40 percent. Some reduction in interest rates since 1982 has reduced that percentage, but it would still be very high in relation to figures of 10 years ago. Moreover, other significant points are the changed lending practices, such as mortgages in which interest rates adjust in line with general changes in interest rate levels, or short-term three- to five-year loans with a balloon payment at the end which would involve refinancing, possibly at higher interest rates. Home buyers going into these arrangements would not be in the same happy position as people in the 70s who were paying off long-term mortgages at low interest rates set many years earlier.

The high cost of servicing home loans through the higher cost of homes and high interest rates limits the scope for future capital gain from further increase in values. At the same time, many people renting homes are now obtaining relatively better value than in earlier years. In a boom there is almost a situation of "the sky is the limit" for capital value of housing, but rental values generally cannot increase much faster than the rate at which average earnings are increasing.

Interesting information and figures on the relative position of owners and renters are contained in an article entitled "The Condominium Trend: The Response to Inflation," by Theodore Crone in the March/April 1983 issue of *Business Review*, published by the Federal Reserve Bank of Philadelphia. The article points out that in 1984 marginal tax rates will be about 20 percent below their 1980 level. These lower marginal tax rates reduce the taxation benefits of owning somewhat. Lower inflation may also have a similar effect.

Tables included in the article show that on certain assumptions of lower tax rates and lower inflation it could take home owners four years to recover the cost of investing in their home, compared with two years under conditions which prevailed in the 70s.

In considering the relative merits of renting and buying, people with relatively low income and family commitments should remember one vital fact. It is that however pleasant it may be to see medium- to long-term capital gain on the value of a home, you cannot use future capital gain to buy food or pay your bills. Even the most sophisticated electronic check-out equipment will not accept future capital gain to pay for the groceries.

As the advantages of owning in the years ahead are not likely to be as clear-cut as in earlier years, every couple should consider this question carefully and do their arithmetic. If you have to move, for career reasons or family reasons, soon after purchasing a home, the capital gain may not be sufficient to offset the costs of buying and selling. These costs can often total between 6 and 9 percent of the value of the home and an even greater percentage of the purchaser's equity, comprised of the down payment and a small component of capital repayment in the mortgage installments in the first few years.

People who feel that one or more moves in the next 5 to 10 years is a distinct possibility may be more inclined to rent. So too would those who find better value for their housing dollar in renting, especially if their resources are limited. On the other hand, those with more adequate capital who can cope with the relatively high costs of carrying housing mortgages these days, or can get into the house and area for which they have a strong preference only by buying, would be more attracted to buy rather than rent.

Further Information

One of the useful booklets published by the Money Management Institute (a subsidary of Household International of Prospect Heights, Illinois) is entitled "Your Housing Dollar." It discusses the management of housing dollars; housing needs; deciding where you want to live; the alternatives of renting, buying, or building; the use of specialist services; how to judge housing; and how to finance buying or building. There are also comments on title search, insurance, and how to plan a move.

Personal Money Management

The concluding chapters of the book move into the area of personal money management. It could be argued that the last chapter dealing with the investment aspects of owning a home and the relative merits of renting and buying under present conditions should be in Part 6 dealing with money management. It was included in the investment section, but the comments in that chapter would certainly be relevant in relation to personal money management discussed in succeeding chapters.

33

The Essentials of Sound Money Management

There is an old Scottish saying that any fool can make money, but it takes a wise person to save it. Another old English philosopher made the comment that an income of £20 a year and an expenditure of £19 a year meant happiness, but an income of £200 a year and an expenditure of £210 a year meant misery.

A more recent quip which is relevant to this area is the cynic's definition of bank finance as the funds which a banker (or perhaps any other type of lender) will readily lend to you once you have proved to him conclusively that you don't really need them.

Adapting Lessons from Corporate Financial Management

Corporate finance people have given a lot of attention over many years to financial management—to the effective use of funds, the raising of funds as economically as possible, to making use of borrowed funds without exposing the business to undue risk, to various means of controlling the use of financial resources throughout the business. This is obviously a very broad subject, but the essentials of corporate financial management could be summarized in five basic requirements. The first is to ensure that there is an adequate base of permanent risk capital (common or preferred stocks) The second is to match long-term assets with long-term sources of funds, either capital funds that are semipermanent or long-term loan funds. The third requirement is to raise the right type of funds at the right time and on the right terms. The next is to ensure that there is a balanced spread of maturities of liabilities so that the tasks of repayment or refinancing of different liabilities do not occur about the same time. The fifth requirement is to keep fixed commitments in terms of interest or leasing charges, etc., to reasonable levels which would not lead to financial embarrassment in difficult times.

In many ways, sound personal money management involves adopting and modifying those requirements to suit the personal situation.

Eight Steps to Sound Money Management

The most significant eight steps to sound personal money management could be summarized as follows:

1. Buildup of capital as quickly as possible in the early days of earning income to provide a base for future financial security.
2. Conserve what you have and seek protection against various hazards through insurance, making use of term life insurance which provides high cover at low cost without any of the associated benefits of loan value, surrender value, and so on; disability insurance to guard against the loss of income through sickness or injury; health insurance as protection against major medical expenses; and insurance of assets such as home, motor vehicle, and so on.
3. Make judicious but effective use of credit and borrowed funds.
4. Invest wisely.
5. Set long-term goals and review progress in achieving them from time to time.
6. Set a definite plan which is regularly reviewed.
7. Use effective but practical budgeting.
8. Make sensible use of tax planning without allowing the taxation tail to wag the sound money management dog (see comments in Chapter 9 and elsewhere in the text).

If that recipe for sound money management is followed, most people would achieve as sound a financial position as is practicable in their circumstances and avoid many of the problems and heartbreaks of financial difficulties.

Many of the above points are discussed in more detail in this and later chapters.

Effective and Practical Budgeting

Most people would agree that budgeting helps to control money matters. But there are many people who are not using budgeting effectively in their money management—perhaps because they never got around to it, perhaps because they soon became frustrated with an overly complicated budget and lost all interest, perhaps because they did not know the right way to go about it.

If budgeting is to be used effectively in personal money management, it should include the following features:

1. *Realistic.* Aim for the happy medium between the two extremes— one of making it so tight that it cannot be achieved, and the other extreme of being so generous that there is no real incentive for tighter control of money.
2. *Complete.* See that all expenses are covered, including those that happen quite infrequently, perhaps several years apart, such as replacement of major appliances, repainting of home, etc.
3. *Balance.* It should be specific enough to give reasonably detailed control without being so detailed and complex that keeping it up-to-date is a massive task.
4. *A graduated approach.* Think first of the major categories of expenses including those which are fixed and those which are variable, those which are paid weekly or monthly and those which are paid quarterly, half-yearly, or yearly. Then go into the subgroupings within the broad groups, for example, vegetables, meat, fruit, etc., in the food category.
5. *Timing of expenditure.* Make suitable arrangements through use of special bank accounts or some other way so that funds will be available to meet the relatively large costs which occur at quarterly, half-yearly, yearly, or less frequent intervals.
6. *Review.* Have a quick look at the budget at about monthly intervals and a more detailed review half-yearly or yearly.
7. *Relative priorities.* Make decisions based on your sense of values as to allocation of income for payments to schools, churches, and community or political organizations.

Further Information

In the money management library published by the Money Management Institute, a subsidiary of Household International of Prospect Heights, Illinois, there are two booklets with a good deal of useful information and comments on the subject matter of this chapter. One is "Your Financial Plan." and the other is "Reaching Your Financial Goals."

34

The Wise Use of Credit and Borrowed Funds

There is a story of a Texan oil millionaire who had been in the habit of carrying very large amounts of currency with him and paying for everything in cash. After a large amount of cash was stolen from him, a sales representative for one of the oil companies persuaded him to apply for a credit card some years ago when credit cards were just being introduced. The elation of the sales representative in signing up such a good potential customer turned to dismay when the credit department informed him, so the story goes, that a credit card could not be issued because they were unable to find any previous credit history for the applicant.

The point was made in an earlier chapter that some cynics described bank finance as the funds which the banker will readily lend to you once you prove to him conclusively that you really do not need it. That definition and the story about the credit card are a reminder that wise use of credit and the maintenance of a good credit rating are an essential part of personal money management today.

The Cost of Underuse and Overuse of Credit and Borrowing

In referring to underuse and overuse of credit and borrowing, we are looking at underuse or overuse in relation to a prudent use of these facilities. Those who make less than normal use of credit and borowing could be denying themselves and their spouses and families the benefits of a better home, or their own home, or of appliances, automobiles, or other assets. Underuse of credit and borrowing facilities may also mean missing out on the opportunities to build up capital through investments, especially in real estate, that would otherwise not be possible, and also missing out on the leverage or multiplying effect of borrowing on those investments. It could also mean missing out on the benefits in times of inflation of borrowing 1973 dollars and paying part of the debt off in 1983, 1993, or 2003 dollars, which are a considerably lower real value in terms of purchasing power. It could also mean missing out on the tax benefits which prudent borrowing may make possible.

Turning the overuse of credit, the extreme cost of overuse would be bankruptcy or severe financial distress. Even if overuse does not lead to that extreme result, it may mean the loss of assets that have to be sold to meet liabilities. It can also mean the dissipation of too much of one's earnings on interest, including the much higher interest rates which generally have to be paid by those who make excessive use of credit and borrowing and hence would not qualify for relatively low risk funds. Apart from the financially measurable results, there may be serious effects in terms of tension leading to possible health problems, perhaps marriage breakup, or problems with children in a situation where home life becomes unstable because of clamoring creditors.

Obviously, the sensible course is to find a happy medium between the two extremes of little or no use of credit on the one hand and excessive, irresponsible use of credit on the other.

Some Basic Principles

Broadly, the sensible approach to use of credit or borrowing is to make use of these facilities to make possible the enjoyment of assets, whether home, appliances, automobiles, or other items, earlier than would otherwise have been possible without going to the extreme of developing a "champagne" appetite on a "beer" income. Credit and borrowing facilities could also be used to make better use of resources including the equity in a home, to build up capital through wise investment, or for other worthwhile uses.

Any particular use of credit or borrowing has to be considered in relation to existing liabilities and current income level. Obviously, it would make more sense to use credit or to borrow when total liabilities are low in relation to net worth and commitments to pay interest and repay debts are not high in relation to current earnings.

As a general principle, it is wise to keep credit repayments for consumer type credit on purchase of automobiles, appliances, and so forth to no more than about 15 percent of disposable income, that is, income after allowing for tax. (For some people currently paying up to 35 or 40 percent of their income to meet mortgage payments, an even smaller proportion may be appropriate.)

Another important point is to ensure that any new commitment can be fitted into your overall expenditure budget while still leaving a portion of the income available as a reserve in case of sudden, unexpected increase in expenditure or decrease in income. It is also wise, wherever possible, to retain some portion of potential capacity for borrowing and use of consumer credit to meet any unexpected emergencies.

Building Up and Maintaining a Good Credit Rating

Years ago parents of adolescent children used to worry about the best way of telling them the facts of life. Today their major worry is how to get them started in the wise use of credit and the building up of a credit rating.

To avoid the situation faced by the Texan millionaire in the story at the beginning of this chapter and other people experiencing difficulty in their first application for a loan (perhaps a housing loan) simply because there is no credit history since they had previously paid cash, it is a good plan to encourage children to gradually build up their credit rating as soon as they are old enough to cope with a credit account. It may be wise to encourage them to open a credit account with a local store when they first start earning some part-time income. A good history of paying the account promptly with that store can then help them in obtaining credit elsewhere for larger amounts as they move into the work force and have need for larger amounts of credit or borrowed funds for housing loans or other major purposes.

Once you have established a credit rating, it is a good plan to ensure that you maintain it. If you run into difficulties, through health problems, unemployment, or other unexpected causes, you should make a determined effort to apply the principles discussed in the remainder of this chapter to the problem as quickly as possible. If you can see that an account or an installment cannot be paid in time, it is generally better to contact the creditor and see if it is possible to arrange some temporary deferment or rescheduling of the debt.

An Early Warning System for Possible Cash Crises

Experienced finance people say that the best time to raise capital or loan funds is before you need them. In personal money management, you can generally arrange finance more readily and on more favorable terms before serious problems arise rather than after. So this makes it necessasry to try to look out for early signs of possible problems—perhaps signs of production cutbacks in the industry in which you are working, business changes which may affect your income, signs of increasing interest rates which may add to your expenditure, or any other matter which could have a significant effect on your financial situation. The person who is fully committed with little in the way of cash reserves and little ability to build up savings out of income has to be even more vigilant in this regard.

The aim should be to try to foresee difficulties of the type referred to above at least a few months in advance so that you have time to do something about them. This may sometimes necessitate arranging temporary loans, perhaps at relatively high interest rates, to give you some time in which to rearrange your finances on loans at somewhat lower interest rates and better overall terms.

If you see the possibility of troubled financial times ahead, it may be wise to seek advice from a financial counselor or a counselor at your place of employment, if such services are available, or perhaps advice from a person in the family or circle of friends who is in finance or banking, or a business person who is more versed in these matters than you are.

Intensive Care Approach for Dealing with Emergencies

If the early warning approach discussed above works effectively, you may be able to eliminate or at least minimize cash emergencies. But if it seems that an emergency is imminent, then you have to apply a sort of intensive care approach. In hospitals these days, people with serious heart ailments and other major problems are placed in an intensive care ward. Their condition is monitored through instruments and computers with alarm systems which will bring specialist medical assistance to them very quickly when it is needed.

In personal money management emergencies, it is necessary to adopt something like this philosophy so that top priority can be given to trying to deal with the emergency.

One possibility worth considering is whether you may be able to refinance the mortgage on your home to make additional funds available. This has been a relatively painless way out of financial emergencies for people whose equity in their home has grown considerably both through repayment of part of the original debt and an increase in house values.

In this sort of situation, realism must be the keynote to action. You have to accept that a little harsh medicine may appear unpalatable now, but it may be a good deal more pleasant (or less unpleasant) than considerably harsher medicine that may be needed later. It is dangerous to fall into the trap of hoping that something will turn up to save you from taking some unpleasant action.

To some extent, the other important factor in addition to realism is adopting the right psychological attitude. It is well to remember the old saying about the person who thought he was badly off because he had no shoes until he met a person who had no feet. If an actual or incipient emergency arises, the process of "trading down" (selling your home and moving to a less valuable home with lower mortgage and other costs, or the sale of an automobile and the purchase of an older, less expensive model) may not be easy to take, but it is not the end of the world. In this sort of problem, as in others that may occur in other areas, it helps if you are prepared to visualize the worst possible situation that could eventuate and then train yourself and others in the family to accept the fact that if it does eventuate you can live with it.

Perhaps trading down, the sale of other assets, or seeking temporary financial arrangements may mean that the worst possible situation will not eventuate. However, if you have made up your mind that if it does eventuate it can be accepted, you have taken a significant step in the right direction. Indeed, once you have made that step you are more likely to ensure that the worst possible situation does not eventuate, because you will then be prepare to make the unpleasant decisions which you previously may have been hesitant to make.

Further Information

Like the preceding chapters, this chapter closes with a reference to useful information and comments in another booklet in the Money Management Library published by Money Management Institute, a subsidiary of Household International of Prospect Heights, Illinois. The booklet, entitled "Managing Your Credit," covers subjects such as what consumer credit is, the pros and cons of credit and its cost, creditworthiness, comparing credit charges, types of consumer credit, sources of credit and details of credit arrangements, circumstances under which credit could be used, shopping for credit, and handling financial difficulties.

35

Providing for Later Years

A cynic has said that, because of inflation, after working for many years to build up a nest egg, he found that when he eventually got to retirement it was only chicken feed. Today, with longer life expectancy and a growing number of people retiring from their normal occupations at a relatively young age, the question of providing for retirement and later years is significant for most people. It involves long-term preparations, making best use of tax benefits, preparation as retirement approaches, and sound personal money management in retirement years.

Long-Range Preparation

The best time to start preparing for retirement in later years is the day on which you commence to earn income, however young that may be. The action you take in those early years in relation to sound money management and wise investment may have a significant effect on the amount of your capital when you reach retirement and the extent to which you can enjoy financial security and freedom from worry in later years.

Essentially, the long-term preparation consists of applying the principles of sound personal money management and wise investment which have been discussed throughout this book. In particular, there is a need to have definite financial plans, including provision for later years, to protect yourself from hazards by use of life insurance, disability or income protection insurance, and insurance of home and other assets; the wise use of credit and borrowing; maximizing tax advantages available on some types of investments without facing undue risk; and the development of a sound investment policy and a strategy for putting it into effect based on the realities of the investment scene rather than widespread fallacies.

Pensions and Retirement Plans—IRA and Keogh Retirement Accounts

One way individuals can help to make provision for their retirement years is through participation in pension plans provided by employers. The Employee's Retirement Income Security Act of 1974 has limited but useful powers to protect the interests of members of these funds. The booklet "Your Savings and Investment Dollar" published by the Money Management Institute, a subsidiary of Household International of Prospect Heights, Illinois, suggests (on page 19) that prospective employees should ask a number of questions about the plans offered by prospective employers. These questions should relate to any powers for amendment or discontinuance of the plan, and guarantees for life, ability to name beneficiaries, the amount of monthly payments and retirements, the way in which pension funds are invested, benefits on disability and death prior to retirement, the extent to which benefits from amounts contributed would be received in the event of resignation before retirement, any benefits to spouse and dependents on death of a member of the fund after retirement, and any adequate group life insurance plan.

The 1974 legislation (often known by its initials ERISA) allows people not covered by any pension plan to set up Individual Retirement Accounts (IRA). Provided the particular amount is approved by the government, payment of federal taxes on amounts of up to $2,000 per year out of the salary or earnings of self-employed people can be deferred. Tax is payable on withdrawal of the money (which can be done after the age of 59½ without penalty). The tax cost should then be lower, because most individuals would then be in a lower tax bracket after retirement. Withdrawals must commence by the age of 70¼.

Self-employed people may contribute to Keogh Retirement Accounts up to 15 percent of earnings, or a maximium of $15,000. Individuals operating Keogh accounts may also open an IRA account, provided combined total contributions do not exceed $17,000.

After pointing out that there is a wide range of government-approved IRA accounts, including savings and loan associations, banks, credit unions, insurance companies, mutual funds, and security brokers, the booklet goes on to advise those considering these plans to read the terms, including the fine print, carefully.

Answers to questions about the economic merits of etablishing IRA accounts can be obtained from the Public Affairs Staff (160, Pension Guarantee Corporation, 2020 K Street, N.W., Washington, D.C. 20006). Answers to tax questions can be obtained from the local internal revenue office or district taxation office.

As well as those specific retirement investment schemes with tax benefits, tax shelters such as property investments, subject to careful consideration and limitation of risk to which capital is exposed, would also help in maximizing the amount of capital available on retirement.

Preparation as Retirement Approaches

In the three to five years before retirement, it is wise to gradually phase into a more defensive investment policy than what was appropriate in early years. A gradual reduction in the degree of risk to which the portfolio is exposed would be appropriate. This is a wise move because as an individual approaches the retirement stage the facility of rebuilding capital after any adverse investment experience out of future earnings may not be available.

During this period, it may be wise to reduce borrowing so that fixed commitments after retirement will be lower. Any investments of which the income can be deferred until after retirement when the tax rate is likely to be lower (on a lower total income) could also be considered.

Personal Money Management in Retirement

Except for people with very large capital, or income from some other source, personal money management in retirement would generally have to be considerably more defensive than in earlier years. Budgets should be revised to allow for the changed income situation and the probably different spending pattern in retirement.

Retired people should be wary of the inflation mongers. These are sales people for various types of investments who paint an extremely black picture of possible future inflation—perhaps illustrated by examples of what bread, milk, and other staple food items could cost in 10 or 15 years' time on the basis of high inflation rates. Then, somewhat like the "fire and brimstone" preacher of earlier years, they promise you that salvation lies in buying gold, a particular mutual fund, a real estate investment scheme, or whatever else they are selling.

Though inflation cannot be ignored, there are no grounds for believing that inflation in the years ahead will be anything like as high as it was in the 1970s and early 80s (a period when an increase of about 3,000 percent in the price of oil was a very significant nonrecurring factor).

Even more so in retirement years than in earlier times, it is necessary to fully consider the risk of capital loss in any investment designed to produce capital gain—and the need to separate actual money from maybe money.

36

Should Long-Term Debts Be Paid Off Early?

"When I die, I don't care what they write about me as long as it includes the statement that I died a debtor of the organization that gave me a long-term loan at very low interest rates many years ago!" That comment by a businessman was his way of saying that he did not intend to pay off a long-term loan on which the interest rate was a fraction of the going rate during the last few years.

Factors to Be Considered

Many people who are prudent and do not like the idea of having debts (because they or their parents lived through the difficult days of the Depression in the 1930s) are inclined to pay off long-term debts as quickly as possible to "get them off their backs." These people are inclined to apply any lump sum received from sources such as legacies, or the payment from a pension fund on moving to new employment, in reduction of debts.

If you were to apply the principles of sound personal money management, there are a number of factors which need to be considered in relation to this question. They include interest rates both current and prospective; the impact of taxation on interest earnings and interest payments; the level of inflation currently and an estimate of future inflation; alternative investments available, including those that may offer capital gain or provide a tax shelter, such as the IRA and Keogh accounts referred to in the previous chapter; and the cash need of the individual during the years ahead.

All of the above factors need to be considered carefully. For example, if the interest rate you are paying on a loan is much higher than the rate which you could earn by investing money elsewhere rather than repaying the loan, then at first glance this would be a reason for using the funds to repay the loan. But if the interest you are paying is an allowable deduction for tax purposes and you would pay a high rate of tax on any interest earnings, the difference on an after-tax basis may be much lower.

Even if the after-tax figures suggest there would be a case for using funds to repay the loan, other information may change the picture. You would have to think seriously about repaying in 1984 dollars a debt which you could repay in 1994 dollars or 2004 dollars, which would probably have a significantly lower real value in terms of purchasing power (even though inflation in the next 10 to 20 years will probably be considerably lower than it was in the 70s and early 80s).

As for alternative investments, if funds which you have available can be used in investments which afford good scope for capital gain, providing a large overall return and significant tax benefits, or if you can invest in tax shelters, or in IRA or Keogh accounts, those alternatives may be preferable.

Finally, your liquid position, to use the financial term, that is, your position in terms of cash, term deposits, or other investments which can be turned into cash readily, has to be considered. If your cash resources are faily low and/or there is a probable need for a significant amount of cash in the near future for purchase of a home or prolonged foreign travel, assistance to other members of the family, or whatever, then repayment may not make much sense. There is not much point in using funds now available to repay a long-term debt ahead of time and then suddenly have to seek to borrow funds a little later. This is particularly important if rising interest rates or tightening of the money supply could mean that the loan funds you may need later on may be more costly and more difficult to obtain.

Making Decisions in Particular Cases

To make a decision in a particular case as to whether to repay a long-term loan early, you would need to do your arithmetic in relation to the factors discussed above. The first step would be to calculate the after-tax interest cost on the interest you are now paying. You would compare that with the after-tax interest earnings if you invest the funds elsewhere. You would then need to take into account not only the current rate of inflation but estimates for the years ahead (taking the figures from reliable economic sources, and not from the inflation mongers who may be exaggerating possible inflation to sell a particular type of investment).

You would then need to consider what alternative investments are available other than simply investing in the fixed interest area. These alternatives could include equity investments, which may offer prospects for capital gain and tax benefits; tax shelters, including investment in real estate propositions with reasonable use of borrowed funds; and the tax shelter benefits of IRA for Keogh accounts.

Naturally, in considering alternative investments, it would not be a matter of considering all of the wide range of investments available at a particular time. Consideration would have to be limited to those which were appropriate to the investment policy and situation of the individual investor. For example, if a person has limited capital, limited income from other sources, or is retired, there is no opportunity of rebuilding capital after any adverse investment experience. Some investments that may be attractive to other people because they offer prospects of capital gain may not be suitable because of the risk involved. In that event, such a person's consideration would be limited to the investments that are a practical alternative to him or her, which may include fixed interest investments and perhaps limited investment in the equity area (together with use of the tax advantages on IRA or Keogh accounts).

In looking at present and possible future cash needs, it would be necessary to allow for contingencies and possible major cash needs arising sometime in the future which cannot be foreseen right now.

If there is a big after-tax difference between the interest being paid and possible interest earnings, if estimated inflation rates for the next 5 to 10 years are very low, if the individual is already taking full advantage of IRA or Keogh accounts, if he or she has no major cash needs in the near future and, from a policy viewpoint, other equity type investments are not appropriate, then there could be a case for using at least part of the funds now available to repay long-term debts ahead of time.

At the other extreme, if the gap between the after-tax interest earnings and payment rates is not great, if the investor could take advantage of other alternatives including tax shelters or investments offering good prospects of capital gain, or if inflation was expected to be 5 to 10 percent per annum or more, then there would be a case for not using the funds to repay long-term debts ahead of time.

Keeping Your Options Open and Partial Early Repayments

If an investor is uncertain as to whether to use funds to repay long-term debts ahead of time, it may be wise, as a first step, to refrain from using the funds in that way. In the phrase used so often by politicians, this leaves his or her options open because he/she could still make a decision later to use the funds for early repayment of the long-term debt. On the other hand, if the investor makes the repayment now and utilizes all or most of the available funds in that way and subsequently finds that he or she needs cash or that there are alternative investments available that are more appealing, he/she cannot go back to the lender an ask him to reverse the transaction. He or she may also find it not so easy to obtain funds from other sources because of monetary conditions or interest rates.

Another alternative in the event of doubt as to which is the right course to follow is to use the step system. In that event, part of the funds could be used for repayment of some of the debts ahead of time while the balance could be used for some other purpose. Then the matter could be reviewed from time to time in the light of changing interest rate conditions or changes in any other factors discussed above.

37

Conclusion

Many years ago when bikini swimsuits were first becoming popular, a nearsighted visitor from the country, mistaking the undulating stripes on the bikinis for arrows, said, "Good heavens! What they don't show, they point to." The material in this book may not show all the answers to investment and money management planning, but it should point the way to successful programs in those areas.

Years ago a preacher in one of the southern states who was training his assistant in how to deliver sermons said, "First of all, you tells 'em what you're going to tell 'em, then you tells 'em what you have just told 'em." Applying that principle, we now turn to a brief summary of the contents of the book followed by a listing of some terms (including some which are lighthearted) to illustrate some of the important points.

A Brief Summary

In investment, as in education, there is a case for returning to the three Rs. In investments the three Rs are return, risk, and relativity. It is also necessary to recognize fallacies such as the hedge against inflation fallacy, the fallacy that property values never go down, and the efficient market fallacy.

In considering return on investment, it is necessary to take into account the time value of money and the difference between the actual money of income return and the maybe money of capital gain, and to understand the sources of capital gain as well as the impact of taxation and changing interest rates on investment. As for risk in investing, it is necessary to consider less obvious sources of risk such as market risk, accounting and information risk, the cyclical movements in markets, and the herd instinct of investors. Various investments should be seen in relation to their risk category and how they could fit into the degree to which various types of investors can expose themselves to risk. It is essential that risk be recognized and controlled in the selection of investments and the reviewing of portfolios.

As for relativity, investments are no exception to the general principle that matters can be seen more clearly when they are related to some standard. By the use of the opportunity cost concept, which is widely used in business management, it is possible to calculate the relative cost for equity type investments compared with fixed interest investments. Research has shown that there is a significant difference between the results of equity investments made when the relative cost is low compared with those made at higher levels. Research also shows that there is a big difference between actual achievement of capital gain in the stock markets and popular misconceptions on this subject.

In applying the three Rs of investing, it is necessary to have a policy suited to the individual and the strategy for putting that policy into effect. This involves a recognition of market cycles, market fashions, and the importance of timing in investments. Equity investments such as common stock and real estate call for a study of market cycles, the indicators of possible declines and recoveries, and the need to manage and review portfolios with judicious selling to preserve profits, cut losses, and reduce the vulnerability of a portfolio.

Personal money management calls for recognition of the investment aspects of the purchase of a home, the relative merits of renting and buying under current conditions, the basic principles of sound money management, the wise use of credit and borrowing, the need to make adequate provision for future years, and a sensible approach to considering whether long-term debts should be paid off early.

Some Investment Terms Worth Remembering

Set out below are a number of investment terms which may be worth remembering. Some of them are slightly off-beat definitions which may help to highlight a particular aspect of investment practice. Further information on the relevant terms could be found in the text through the index. They are classified under different groupings.

Behavior of Markets
Point of previous gladness—An offbeat approach based on a ditty about the problem of communicating thoughts from the head of a long-bodied dachshund to its other end. The last two verses of the ditty are "so it

happened while its eyes were filled with tears of sadness, its little tail kept wagging on because of previous gladness." In investments the point of previous gladness is the point prior to which stock would need to have been purchased for the investor to be ahead at the present time.

Disenchantment index. An offbeat index derived from the point of previous gladness on the formula that $D = \sqrt{N - 1}$ where D equals the disenchantment index and N equals the number of months back to the point of previous gladness. There are psychological and mathematical reasons for this formula. The psychological one is that most formulae seem to have a square root sign in them, so it had to go in. The mathematical reason is that there is some problem with the square root of -1, so N had to go in. More seriously, if a realistic disenchantment index could be devised, it could be significant, because markets find it much more difficult to recover when sustained declines cause serious disenchantment (for example, the disenchantment in relation to the gold market which at the beginning of 1984 was over 50 percent below its price of four years earlier).

Market rating. The rating of a stock or an investment in a market in terms of its price on the basis of dividend yield or price earnings multiple related to the market average. A change in the market rating over a period from, say, 1½ to 2½ can cause a significant further increase in price in addition to that reflecting improved earnings. A reduction from a previously excessive market rating would accentuate the extent of a decline reflecting decreased earnings, or offset part of the gain that may have accompanied increased earnings.

Off the boil. In the latter stages of a boom, the market often "goes off the boil" for some months, declining from an earlier peak and failing to recover for several months. As booms and bull markets need to maintain momentum, a market that has been off the boil for more than four to six months is generally, but not inevitably, a market headed for a cyclical slump (possibly from a slightly higher peak in a last flutter).

Herd instinct. The tendency for institutions, mutual funds, and professional investors to rush into or out of markets at about the same time. It is this force which has been behind most significant booms from the South Sea Bubble over 200 years ago.

Normal trading range. An estimate of the range within which trading will take place in the future based on an extension of the medium-term trend line joining the bottoms of downswings, and an upper line parallel to that line which borders an area within which most trading has taken place for most of the time over several years. This is a useful but by no means infalliable indicator of the area in which trading could be expected in the future.

Expectation index. An index to measure the relative amount of anticipation or overanticipation ("blue sky") in a market in terms of the chances, on the basis of past experience, of achieving adequate capital gain. It is arrived at by dividing the failure rate in achieving that amount of adequate capital gain in the past by the success rate.

Bigger fool theory. This theory states that in a boom, it can be profitable to buy at a foolish price because before too long a bigger fool will come along and offer you an even more foolish price. The problem is that in a finite world the supply of fools is not limitless, and the smart thing is to be no later than the next-to-last fool when the crunch comes and the market goes into a slump.

Market study. A study of market movements using some concepts used by chartists, such as the concept of support and resistance, and trend analysis, which discards the chartist's theory that certain patterns are sure to be followed by certain price movements. Market study also includes the use of estimated normal trading ranges described above.

The just right syndrome. The view that a stock market or other market should rise because of declining interest rates, improved economic conditions, or other factors, incorrectly assuming that the market now is just right. In fact, markets have a tendency to be well away from what would be the just right situation for most of the time.

Fallacies

Among the terms which are relevant in the area of fallacies are the following:

The inflation hedge fallacy. The fallacy that certain investments provide assured and sustained capital gain, which would mean that they can be bought with confidence at any time and at any price. There is no such thing as an inflation hedge because of the statement attributed to Abraham Lincoln that you cannot fool all of the people all of the time.

The Abraham Lincoln approach to market study. The statement quoted above which was attributed to Abraham Lincoln could be adapted to market trends by saying that you can have sharply rising trends for a relatively short period, gradually rising trends for a relatively long period, but you cannot have sharply rising trends for a long period.

Actual money and maybe money. It is necessary to distinguish between the actual money such as dividend or interest receipts, net rental receipts on property investments, and the actual expenditure on investments, from the maybe money of capital gain—particularly relevant for persons contemplating the purchase of a home or other investments, who should remember this point: however pleasant it may be to enjoy medium- to long term-capital gain, you cannot buy food or pay bills with it. There has yet to be invented check-out equipment at supermarkets which could enable you to use that future capital gain to pay for the groceries. (In the medium term, refinancing of the house mortgage against an increasing equity in the home may solve the problem in part, but high interest rates and legal and other costs associated with refinancing can be problems.)

The law of gravity. Because the law of gravity has not been repealed, market rises are almost inevitably followed by declines.

Hangover analogy. Claims that markets are sure to recover a short while after a decline from a previously rapid rise ignore the hangover analogy. This analogy is that just as a long party tonight can mean a worse headache tomorrow, so a long or hectic boom can be followed by a longer and more severe slump.

The replacement costs fallacy. The claim that property values must rise because of increasing replacement costs is incorrect because it assumes that market values are set by some cost plus formula related to current replacement costs. In fact, they are determined by supply and demand, and there have been many occasions including recent years when increasing replacement costs have been accompanied by declining property values in reaction to a previous boom.

Bargain sales and some tax shelter schemes. It has been said that bargain sales are what some people go to to save more money than they can afford. Similarly, some people are inclined to spend more money in some doubtful tax shelter schemes than they can really afford.

The going broke gracefully syndrome. Some traditionalists who are not prepared to recognize changing times in various industries are said to be determined to go broke gracefully. The reliance of some investors and investment specialists on blue chip stocks, which have proved so disappointing in recent years, could be the stock market equivalent of that philosophy.

Efficient markets fallacy. There is a view widely held in some educational institutions and some sections of the investment business that because information about stock markets is widely publicized, the market at any time represents a reasonably efficient estimate of the value of the stocks. Hence, according to this theory, nothing is to be gained by studying the timing of moves into or out of the market or in selection of particular stocks. The fact is that markets are inefficient and have been growing more inefficient because of the increasing amount of speculation, both local and foreign, and the herd instinct referred to above.

Simplifying Assumption Salvation (SAS). Distressed mariners are saved by the SOS signal, but distressed theoreticians in relation to the efficient markets fallacy are saved by the SAS (simplifying assumption salvation). Choosing the right simplifying assumption can make any theory look respectable. College students tell the story of three shipwrecked professors discovering a sealed can containing food and some explosives. While the engineering professor claims that his skills are needed to determine the forces needed to open the container and the professor of chemistry insists that it is his knowledge of the chemical properties of explosives which will be needed, the professor of economics tells them to save their time as he will solve the problem simply by assuming that they have a can opener.

Relativity

In relation to the concept of relativity in investing, the following terms may be useful reminders:

Opportunity cost. In a lighthearted vein, opportunity cost of bottles of beer available to Australian servicemen on a tropical base in World War II was not the low price of about 12 cents at which they could buy it but the $2 per bottle offered for it by American troops in a neighboring camp. More seriously, opportunity cost in the investment world is the income foregone by following one particular investment path. For equities the elements in the opportunity cost are the income foregone (the yield gap), the transaction costs, and the additional risks involved, especially risk of market fluctuation compared with other investments.

Relative cost. The cost of common stock or other equity investment compared with fixed interest investments, being an application of the opportunity cost concept designed to calculate the amount that would have to be invested in common stocks or other equities to produce the same income return as could be earned from the investment of $1 in fixed interest investments. It is arrived at by dividing the fixed interest (bond) rate by the dividend yield.

The no change syndrome. The widespread tendency for common stocks to be recommended for buying because dividend yields or price earnings multiples are attractive compared with figures of 10 or 15 years ago. This approach is illogical because there is a vast difference between, for example, a dividend yield of 4 percent in the mid-80s when the fixed interest rate is around 11 to 12 percent and a dividend yield of about 4 percent 15 or 20 years ago when the fixed interest rate was about 4 percent.

Realism gap. The gap between the price of common stocks, real estate, and other equities in recent years and a more realistic price related to earning capacity, cost of money, and returns available on fixed interest investments. This gap means that there is a potential for significant decline if the market, in later years, should return even some of the way back to more realistic price levels.

Miscellaneous

Finally, we turn to terms related to miscellaneous aspects of investment practice.

Definition of an investor. According to a cynic, an investor is a disappointed speculator, that is, a person who bought an investment with the intention of making a quick profit on it, then when the market did not cooperate with his predictions virtuously proclaims that he is a long-term investor and not one of the speculators moving in and out of the market all the time.

Definition of a speculator. A speculator, in the eyes of the conventional investment wisdom, is somebody who is speculating in less prestigious stocks. Large institutions which speculate in blue chips and prestigious stocks describe their speculation as investment.

Hard luck currency. In the years preceding January 1980, gold was described as hard currency—the currency which would be relied on to hold its value as distinct from soft paper currencies which were constantly losing their values as the result of inflation. The fact that in the early months of 1984 the gold price was more that 50 percent below the level of four years earlier would suggest that the title of that investment would have to be changed from hard currency to hard luck currency.

The first law of investment. The best reason for not making a particular investment is not being able to afford it. This is not a criticism of reasonable and prudent use of borrowed funds, but a warning against the danger of excessive or imprudent borrowing to make investments.

Accounting and information risk. The risk that an investment may not turn out as well as expected because of the difference between the real situation and that portrayed by accounting figures in company reports or information provided by some sellers of real estate properties.

Accounting gymnastics. Techniques used by directors of some companies in choosing from the wide range of alternative accounting practices those which would enable them to report a situation close to what they would have liked to happen in the period rather than what actually happened. If accounting gymnastics ever becomes an Olympic sport, the United States, Britain, Canada, Australia, New Zealand, and similar countries could be expected to win a lot of gold medals.

Bottoms up accounting. The practice by which some companies are inclined to decide on the net profit they want to report (the bottom line) for a particular period, set that figure, and then make appropriate adjustments (accounting gymnastics) through the use of favorable accounting techniques to relate that figure to the actual sales revenue for the period.

Cynical definition of accounting. Accounting (the discipline in which I was initially trained) has been defined by a cynic as the art of being excruciatingly precise about a lot of arbitrary assumptions.

Index